BFI FILM CLASSI
. . . .

Rob White
SERIES EDITOR

Colin MacCabe and David Meeker
SERIES CONSULTANTS

Cinema is a fragile medium. Many of the great classic film of the past now exist, if at all, in damaged or incomplete prints. Conce d about the deterioration in the physical state of our film heritage, u lational Film and Television Archive, a Division of the British Film Institute, has compiled a list of 360 key films in the history of the cinema. The long-term goal of the Archive is to build a collection of perfect showprints of these films, which will then be screened regularly at the Museum of the Moving Image in London in a year-round repertory.

BFI Film Classics is a series of books commissioned to stand alongside these titles. Authors, including film critics and scholars, film-makers, novelists, historians and those distinguished in the arts, have been invited to write on a film of their choice, drawn from the Archive's list. Each volume presents the author's own insights into the chosen film, together with a brief production history and a detailed filmography, notes and bibliography. The numerous illustrations have been specially made from the Archive's own prints.

With new titles published each year, the BFI Film Classics series will rapidly grow into an authoritative and highly readable guide to the great films of world cinema.

Could scarcely be improved upon ... informative, intelligent, jargon-free companions.
The Observer

Cannily but elegantly packaged BFI Classics will make for a neat addition to the most discerning shelves.
New Statesman & Society

The final image of *L'Âge d'or* suggests that the Christian symptom is a genocidal hatred of women

BFI FILM CLASSICS

L'ÂGE D'OR

·················

Paul Hammond

 Publishing

First published in 1997 by the
BRITISH FILM INSTITUTE
21 Stephen Street, London W1P 2LN

The British Film Institute exists
to promote appreciation, enjoyment, protection and
development of moving image culture in and throughout the
whole of the United Kingdom.
Its activities include the National Film and
Television Archive; the National Film Theatre;
the Museum of the Moving Image;
the London Film Festival; the production and
distribution of film and video; funding and support for
regional activities; Library and Information Services;
Stills, Posters and Designs; Research;
Publishing and Education; and the monthly
Sight and Sound magazine.

British Library Cataloguing-in-Publication Data
A catalogue record for this book is available from the British Library

ISBN 0–85170–642–8

Designed by
Andrew Barron & Collis Clements Associates

Typesetting by
D R Bungay Associates, Burghfield, Berks.

Printed in Great Britain by Norwich Colour Print

CONTENTS

. . . .

To Ana Forcada

THE FIRST PRISMATIC ARTICULATION
·························

Posters had gone up around the pueblo: 'Scorpions wanted! Top prices paid!' An hour later the fisherfolk of Cadaqués were congregating in the Hotel Miramar, horny hands wrapped around heaving jamjars. That night, 4 April 1930, Luis Buñuel bedded down with fifty of the beasts.

The director, his assistants Jacques Brunius and Claude Heymann, cameraman Albert Duverger and a clutch of actors were on the Costa Brava for five days of location shooting. The 'grandiose geological delirium' of nearby Cap de Creus would be *L'Âge d'or*'s opening backdrop.[1] Dalí country, of course. But where was co-scenarist Salvador?

On the run. The Christmas before, Salvador Dalí Senior, incensed by newspaper reports of his offspring's Surrealist shenanigans in Paris – particularly a picture called 'Sometimes I Spit For Pleasure on My Mother's Portrait' – had banished him from Figueres. Dalí Junior lit out, but by March he was back, looking to buy a fisherman's cottage in Port Lligat, just up the coast from Cadaqués. And from Mum and Dad: the family had a holiday home there. Getting wind of this, the father asked Buñuel to be the go-between: tell my son if he disturbs my peace in Cadaqués I'll stick the Guardia Civil on him. Señor Dalí, a notary, was looked up to in the village, could queer Buñuel's pitch. Appeasement was in order if the location work was to proceed smoothly.

Kept until her death in Ana María Dalí's biscuit tin, *Menjant garotes* (*Eating Sea Urchins*), as the family called the 'vanity movie' Buñuel made that April, is one to add to the filmography. Although it bit into his tight schedule, Buñuel planned the five-minute short with care, having Duverger shoot it on 35mm. The Lumière-style narrative of paterfamilias and spouse strolling through their terraced garden is filmed from eleven different angles. Edited, I'd say, in camera, the movie ends on the cannibal grin of Dalí père as he gobbles a testicular urchin.

Menjant garotes grew out of bloody-minded territorialism and so was not without bearing on what came after. *L'Âge d'or* would begin with an entomological essay on the instinctual behaviour of the scorpion, how it is driven by a primordial will to power. And to self-destruction: was it true that, as an Aragonese folk myth had it, a scorpion encircled by fire stings itself to death?

In the script the scorpion sequence segued into the next, the bandits.[2] The camera would dolly back from an arachnid inching up an

escarpment until the creature was lost to sight. Another angle of the same baked landscape revealed, in medium shot, a bandit clinging to a rock. A match-cut, then, to make the equation: bandit = scorpion.

What with the time spent on *Menjant garotes* and the rain that fell on Cap de Creus, *L'Âge d'or* was soon behind schedule. Either the scorpion sequence wasn't shot, or if it was the creatures were no Rin-Tin-Tins and the footage was unusable. A replacement was needed, and Brunius was dispatched to an agency specialising in pedagogical films, the Compagnie Universelle Cinématographique, to look for it. He came up with *Le Scorpion languedocien*, a popular science documentary made by the Éclair Company in 1912 as part of their 'Scientia' series. The seventy-five 'Scientia' shorts directed by J. Javault and André Bayard between 1912 and 1914 were aimed at schoolkids and focused, in the main, on zoology.

Buñuel had already decided to abrade the look of *L'Âge d'or* by incorporating film shot by other hands. In their functionalist writings on cinema from 1927 to 1929 he and Dalí repeatedly praised scientific documentaries, Fox newsreels and Taylorised Tinseltown productions for their 'anti-artistic' qualities. (*Napoléon*, *Metropolis*, *Le Ballet*

Dalí *père* serves up a sea urchin in *Menjant garotes*, Buñuel's vanity movie of April 1930 (Filmoteca de Catalunya)

mécanique were 'artistic' and, as such, excoriated.) The dilapidated condition of the found print, the way its stuttery framing sometimes fails to keep the asocial scorpions in shot, acts as a foil to Duverger's photogenic camerawork and Buñuel's deft cutting. Getting his state-of-the-art sound film off to a bad start appealed to the director's provocative sense of humour and love of mystification.

The documentary peaks with a rat in a vivarium succumbing to a scorpion's sting, a shot which scuppered the scripted cut matching beast and bandit. The sequence acts instead like a 'prologue', analogous to the eye-slicing scene in *Un Chien andalou*. Although less powerful than that blinding, it's still an effing affront to the viewer. A snare Andalusian.

The prologue tells us that the scorpion's tail 'is formed of a series of five prismatic articulations', and that it 'ends in a sixth vesicular joint, the poison sac'. Since *L'Âge d'or* is also divisible into six discrete parts I've taken my chapter headings from the scorpion intertitles.

On 18 November 1929 the Vicomte de Noailles commissioned Buñuel to make a short of around the same length as *Un Chien* – seventeen minutes – but with sound. At this point Buñuel and Dalí, thinking no further than a remake, again centred their scenario on the tragicomic romancing of a man and a maid. Later, as people like Brunius and Heymann put in their oar, the film grew segmentally from a short into a feature. By February 1930 it was forty-five minutes long and twice the budget. Buñuel now anxiously deferred to his patron-producer, offering to trim things back to the original twenty minutes, but Noailles okayed the longer version. During the March to May shooting further 'gags' were improvised, taking the movie to an hour. Again, the director offered to cut the new material should Noailles say the word. Since nothing *was* deleted, the *ad hoc* work that emerged is as much heterogeneous collage as homogeneous montage. Even well-disposed critics of the time like Jean-Paul Dreyfus – who had a bit part in it – observed that *L'Âge d'or* lacked the formal unity of *Un Chien*. But then, wasn't this Buñuel's goal, to make a film so ragged it couldn't pass, like its predecessor, for being 'well made'?

This collage approach was consonant with the Surrealist intuition that film could replicate the 'dream-work', disguise and derange meaning through a rebus rhetoric of displacement; condensation; accepted contradiction; dislocated time, space and causality. *Mise en scène* and cutting were the elements Buñuel used to 'irrationalise' – 'oneirise'

– Hollywood melodrama. Take the scene in *Un Chien* where a character begins a fall inside a room and ends it in a meadow. Time 'matches', is synchronic; space 'jumps', is diachronic. Buñuel got the idea from looking at Méliès or the Bosetti-Durand school of primitive comedy, I'd wager. Then there's his paradoxical use of the intertitle. 'Sixteen years before', we might read, and in the ensuing shot the actors and the décor haven't changed. Here space is synchronic, time diachronic. I believe Buñuel took this from Keaton. At the end of *The Paleface* (1922) Buster is in a clinch with his girl. Then comes the intertitle 'Two years later'. In the next shot same Buster, same girl, same kiss. With sound to play with, Buñuel took the idea further. In *L'Âge d'or* mis-matches still happen between the 'articulations', through the use of mendacious intertitles; 'matching jump-cuts'; colliding aesthetics and textures. But they also occur within them, by the making of deliberate mistakes in visual or verbal continuity and in having the image perturbed by incongruous sound and word.

As well as functioning oneirically, *L'Âge d'or* is a fine example of Shklovskian 'retardation': the ironical, here permanent, postponement of a climax through the interpolation of incongruous formal and dramatic material. Confound you! Once, though, we've got over the disorientation of a first viewing and look again (and again) we find that the deconstructive tendency is countered by the way recurring details and running jokes hold the film together.

Whether these correspondences were always planned is irrelevant; it's enough that they exist in the eye of the beholder. I'll often submit to my own *délire d'interpretation* in the pages ahead, but right now I'm thinking of the prologue and the 'epilogue': those gruesome scalps of women nailed to a cross amid swirling snow. Brutal death is common to both. Heat counterpoints cold. I see a congruence between the scuttling scorpions in the first shot, long tails stretched out like pokers, limbs bunched at right angles to their abdomens, and the configuration of the

Female trouble: Ernst's praying mantis, cribbed from a photo in Fabre's *Souvenirs entomologiques,* commissioned by Breton in 1924 and printed in the Studio 28 programme

Christian cross in the last. 'The scorpion is a type of arachnid wide-spread in the hot regions of the ancient world,' an intertitle tells us. And what if one of those ancient hot regions was Judaea, *c.* AD30?

Arachnids are phantasmatically linked to femellitude in the male imagination. Witness the Pauline father, St Jerome: 'Woman is the gate of the devil, the road of evil, the sting of the scorpion.' And the Freudian father, Karl Abraham, opining that another arachnid, the spider, represents the feared phallic mother.

We know from the rich lore of the Buñuel family that Luis had a dread of spiders. Nor are scorpions that cuddly. Conchita Buñuel has recounted how their infant sister Margarita, taking the glossy black segments of a scorpion's tail for the beads of a rosary in the garden one day, narrowly missed the fate of the rat in the vivarium.

The intertitles are not Buñuel's work; they came with *Le Scorpion languedocien*. (The lettering was redrawn, of course.) Furthermore, they're verbatim quotations from Jean-Henri Fabre. Immensely popular during the 1910s, especially among children, Fabre's ten-volume *Souvenirs entomologiques* (1898–1907) were the methodological model for the 'Scientia' series. Buñuel, too, was a Fabre enthusiast, having read him as an entomology student in Madrid, and he may have had the insect man in mind when he planned the scorpion sequence. Perhaps this Fabrean analogy had already struck home: 'Two scorpions are often found beneath the same stone, one devouring the other. Is this a case of banditry between equals?'[3] That the Éclair intertitles were straight Fabre doubtless impressed Buñuel as a splendid instance of *hasard objectif*.

Subtitled 'Studies on the Instinct and Manners of Insects', the enthused writings of this outsider scientist – whom Dalí likened to the visionary architect, 'Postman' Cheval – were greatly admired by the Surrealists. Although a deist, the entomologist's austere and terrifying depiction of the dialectic of Eros and Thanatos in nature bears comparison to Sade's atheistic *psychopathia sexualis*. Fabre was especially intrigued by insect courtship. Considering the passivity of the male Golden Gardener beetle towards post-coital evisceration by his mate, he wrote:

> This tolerance reminds one of the scorpion of Languedoc, which on the termination of the hymeneal rites allows the female to devour him without attempting to employ his weapon, the

venomous dagger which would form a formidable defence; it reminds us also of the male of the Praying Mantis, which still embraces the female though reduced to a headless trunk, while the latter devours him by small mouthfuls, with no rebellion or defence on his part.[4]

Although Fabre is nowhere mentioned by name his ideas form the latent content of the film, lending it coherence at the analogical level. *L'Âge d'or* will image the 'hymeneal rites' of a bungling heterosexual couple. The theme of libidinal frustration is even fleetingly announced in the *objet trouvé*. We see a shot of two scorpions, tails entwined in erotic embrace. Suddenly a third arachnid charges through them, sundering the blissful dancers.

THE SECOND PRISMATIC ARTICULATION

Having rejigged the scorpion sequence Buñuel bridged the unforeseen ellipsis between it and the bandits with a perfunctory intertitle: 'Some hours afterwards.' (Another windfall; it comes from *Le Scorpion languedocien*.) The camera focuses on a lone sentinel on a promontory above the sea. On the soundtrack, breaking waves overlaid with Mozart. Dead on his feet, the rag-tag bandit – is it Bill or is it Ben? – uses his Mauser as a crutch, initiating one of the film's many running jokes. The sticks Buñuel's family employed to drum at the local Easter parade were, it's said, fashioned from the crutch of Miguel Pellicero, whose missing leg was restored by the Virgin in the 'Miracle of Calanda' in 1640. The crutch would, of course, become a major signifier in Dalí's paintings.

Then, from the brigand's point of view, a famous but still startling shot of the enemy: four Catholic bishops in full regalia plonked like chessmen on the wave-lapped rocks below, where they drone a glossolalic mass. The curlicues of their crosiers evoke a scorpion tail. Scorpion-catchers from Cadaqués impersonated them. Buñuel scripted insert shots of pious digits marking the place in closed breviaries, thereby setting up another running joke: masturbatory fingers. As the Mozart and mumbles fade from the soundtrack, and the sun-stroked lookout hobbles off to warn his confrères, we may recall the intertitle: 'By no means sociable, [the scorpion] sees off the meddler who disturbs its solitude.'

Who, iconographically, are the 'Scorpion Gang'? Their lowlife status links them, perhaps, to the picaresque novel of Spain's *Siglo de oro*. Could they be kin to the *banditti* of Gothic fiction, or the *bandidos* Goya painted? (Buñuel had scripted a biopic of the artist in 1927.) Their mud-spattered corduroys and espadrilles mark them down as landless labourers. Might they be ciphers for the anarchist 'apostles of the idea' who'd danced on the grave of dictator Primo de Rivera, dead three months after being deposed in January 1930? Given their leader is Max Ernst, do the brigands drolly represent the Surrealist Group itself? Whatever, they're clearly the wretched of the earth, vagabonds, pariahs.

Ernst, a Mabuse clone, snarls and bares his fangs to great effect, barking out commands as he toys with his 'venomous dagger'. Years later he'd claim his collage-novels inspired *L'Âge d'or*, which has a certain truth. It was Ernst who suggested that Eisenstein, in Paris on a stop-over to Hollywood, play a bandit. Buñuel declined, masking his understandable fear of being up-staged by accusing the Russian of prostituting himself on *Romance sentimentale*. The director looked more kindly on Ernst's brother-in-law. Jean Aurenche would have an illustrious career as a scriptwriter – notably for Claude Autant-Lara, Jean Delannoy and Bertrand Tavernier – but in 1930 he had one article to his name. Significantly it was a series of gags, published in the fifth issue of *La Revue du cinéma* (15 October 1929).

In 1931 Aurenche began making advertising films and had the painter repeat his bandit role in *Au petit jour à Mexico*, three minutes long, edited by Brunius, commissioned by 'Meubles Barbès'. Ernst leads a bunch of pistoleros who are about to shoot a hostage until they find he's sat on a Barbès chair. Aurenche's little comedy – Tavernier montaged it into *Clean Slate* (1981) – has been wrongly credited to Buñuel. For Ernst there was another

Bandit iconography: an illustration from one of Dalí's favourite childhood books, Folch i Torres's *The Giant of the Winds* (1911)

spin-off from *L'Âge d'or*: when the bandit set was struck he pounced on the scrimmed plywood walls and painted three pictures on them, including 'Europe After the Rain I' (1933).

The only bandit with a name – 'Péman' – was played by Pierre Prévert. In 1928 Jacques's self-effacing brother co-directed, with Marcel Duhamel, *Souvenirs de Paris*, a documentary shot by Man Ray and J-A Boiffard. Actor and assistant on Cavalcanti's *Le Petit Chaperon rouge* (1929), 'Pierrot' had recently co-scripted a comedy for *Un Chien* star Pierre Batcheff called *Émile, Émile*, but the actor's suicide would stymie the project.

Four of the other five bandits were amigos, artists who, like Buñuel, had left Rivera's stultifying Spain for the cosmopolitan and – given the weakness of the franc – cheap French capital. Francisco Cossío, the brigand with the crutch, arrived there in 1923. Christian Zervos put his painting, Picasso crossed with Matisse, on a par with Ernst's and Miró's. In 1926 he collaborated on Buñuel's theatre production of *El Retablo de Maese Pedro*. Cossío really was lame and limps into shot in *Un Chien*. He'd break with Buñuel after *L'Âge d'or* – 'a counter-revolutionary film,' he said – go back to Spain in 1931 and become a fascist. Juan Esplandiu, the sentinel, came in 1925, shared studio, style and itinerary with Cossío, save that he'd paint posters *for* the Republican cause. These two, plus Buñuel, extraed as smugglers in Jacques Feyder's *Carmen* (1926). Were the grimy bandits a riposte to Feyder's sleek stereotypical Hispanos? After five years' exile Pedro Flores returned to Barcelona in 1933 to teach drawing. Come the civil war, he'd remigrate to Paris. Joaquín Roca (or Roa), another crypto-cubist, seems to have sat out the hostilities in the French capital. Years later, and long after trading paintbrush for guitar, he'd be the white-haired beggar in *Viridiana*.

The odd man out is the bandit who hides his face. Jaume Miravitlles, Dalí's pal at the Marist Brothers school in Figueres, had done time in La Santé for his part in an abortive coup against the Rivera régime by the Catalan nationalist Francesc Macià. Unlike the other Paris School Spaniards, who derided Surrealism, he was friendly with the group. Miravitlles is one of the Marists roped to the donkey-pianos in *Un Chien*. Arriving in Barcelona after *L'Âge d'or*, he lectured there on Surrealism with Crevel and Dalí, and militated in what became the POUM. Between 1936 and 1939 he was Propaganda Commissar for the Catalan Republican government.[5]

The Scorpion Gang are men without women, that much is certain. I take them to be avatars of *Totem and Taboo*'s primordial brotherhood, traumatised by thoughts of the woman-hogging patriarch they've assassinated. They move like automata; the seats of their pants are patched; shirt fronts poke, symptomatically, from unbuttoned flies. Playing a variant of the 'fort-da' game, the dying Péman/Prévert listlessly spools out a rope being tugged through the tines of a pitchfork by Roca and Flores.

The shooting script lets on that this anguishing onanistic ritual was improvised on the day. I see the hand of a great wanker here: Dalí. Sharing a certain homology with the crutch, the pitchfork forms a leitmotif in his wild analysis of Millet's painting 'L'Angélus'.[6] Not long after *L'Âge d'or* Dalí propounded his theory of the 'symbolically functioning' object. The Surrealists would make many of these during the next few years. 'Based on phantasms and representations liable to be provoked by the realisation of unconscious acts',[7] such assemblages of heterogeneous part-objects transmute trauma into fetish and talisman. Their elements may bump and grind – or slither, like the rope through the pitchfork – but to no apparent purpose. Dead erotic, they're a criminal waste of energy.

Framing, lighting, focusing, camera angle, camera movement, movement within the frame, montage are the privileged means cinema has of creating combinations of objects, and part-objects, that can function symbolically in the way Dalí described. If not involuntary, such juxtapositions are often preconscious on the part of the director, cinematographer or set-dresser. Even if the visual field is wholly controlled the spectator may still 'misread' it according to his or her subjective needs.

Louis Delluc took the first faltering step in trying to understand how cinema made the object-world strange, or, more properly, foregrounded its inherent uncanniness. Delluc called it *photogénie*, and built his theory around the insert shot – big close-ups of objects other than the face – after looking at the films of Griffith and De Mille. The essentially mystical idea of *photogénie* became axiomatic for the 20s French avant-garde. Aragon's 'On Décor' (1918), a founding text of Surrealist cinema, toes the Delluc line.[8] After the latter's death in 1924, Jean Epstein picked up the baton. Three years later Buñuel wrote 'On the Photogenic Shot' and cited his ex-teacher:

The miraculous gaze of the lens, silent as paradise, animistic and vital like a religion, humanises beings and things alike. 'On the screen there is no still life. Objects have attitudes,' Jean Epstein, the first to speak to us of this psychoanalytical quality of the lens, has said.[9]

Buñuel was selling himself short here. The idea that *photogénie* brought out the latent, unconscious meaning of objects was more his – and Dalí's – than Epstein's. A Bergsonian theosophist, Epstein had little time for psychoanalysis.

Dalí and Buñuel, though, had been reading Freud since the early 20s, which came in handy when they gate-crashed Surrealism. A journalist visiting Zaragoza in July 1930 found the resting director still at it. Elisabeth Roudinesco has pointed out that the Surrealist poets and painters were the first French intellectuals to value and to *use* Freud, albeit contrariwise, heretically. In the 20s the Surrealist notion of the unconscious was millenial and woolly. Indeed, one might see *L'Âge d'or* as a preamble to the more systematic investigations of the 30s. (In the pages of *Minotaure*, for instance. *Minotaure* was to have been called *L'Âge d'or* in homage to the movie.) The eccentric behaviour the bandits exhibit isn't a symptom of abject morbidity, the film-makers suggest, but of triumphant idealism. Following Rank – Otto, not J Arthur, although he too is ever-present in the movie – Dalí and Buñuel considered that reality's adjustment to the unconscious, and not the other way round, is what marks the true development of humankind.

Péman's last rites are to the golden age of intra-uterine existence. The scene of Cossío trying to sever the umbilical cord is hysterically funny, although you don't necessarily laugh. The gag was, and remained, Buñuel's *modus scenarii*. His first two films are a homage to silent comedy; to the oneiric metalogic and concrete irrationality of Langdon and Keaton. (Like the other Surrealists he'd given up on Chaplin by then.) The somnambulism of the bandits echoes the dizzy, sweet infantilism of Harry Langdon, about whom Buñuel and Dalí were writing enthusiastically in 1929. When the bandit captain orders his men outside the dopes march *away* from the door.

The gags are verbal as well as visual. In an exchange inspired by Benjamin Péret – Buñuel and Dalí's favourite Surrealist poet – Prévert rejects Ernst's exhortation to be up and off with, 'Yes, yes, but you've got

accordions, hippopotami, keys and clinging oaks. ... And paintbrushes.'
Not so daft, given that five of the bandits were painters.

Aside from the Péretesque nonsense, Buñuel intended to give a
cock-and-bull ring to the dialogue by assiduously assembling it in the
wrong order. In the end he toned down the galimatias, although the
diegetic effect remains dyslexic. An example: Esplandiu says 'I've fallen
over, perchance?' Ernst replies, but as if to some other question: 'No,
we haven't seen anything.' This isn't dialogue in the usual sense, but
rather two monologues delivered at cross-purposes. In fine, the kind of
'absolute dialogue' promulgated by the Surrealists in 1928, one that cut
through the politeness of everyday intercourse to discover, in
dysfunctional interlocution, the scintillation of poetic truths. ('Surrealist
dialogue' was inspired by echolalia and the Ganser Syndrome, forms of
verbal hysteria in which the sufferer gives beside-the-point replies.) The
eerie, elliptical quality of the bandit dialogue is enhanced by the inter-
cutting of silent footage – long and medium shots of the hut interior
made at Billancourt studios – with brusque direct sound: talking heads
filmed at Tobis-Klang, shot tight to save on rebuilding the sets. The
pronouncements come from some other place, are already made strange.

Harry Langdon, somnambule bridegroom, in *Long Pants* (1927)   1 7

The phrase 'film sonore et parlant' (sound and talking film), which appears on the credits, laminates *L'Âge d'or* to its time. Sound came late to France, and came from outside. Between March 1929 and July 1930 Tobis-Klangfilm, a Dutch–German combine, challenged the American corporations ERPI (Western Electric) and RCA (General Electric) for control of the French industry. Although unprepared technologically, the French had been debating the relative virtues of *films sonorisés* and *films parlants* since 1928. The feeling was that sound endangered silent montage cinema. Restricted to 'speechless' sound effects montage might survive as the key organising principle. All-talking films – filmed radio – would do it down. Although all sound movies were to mix noise and speech, the compromise 'sound and talking film' is specific to this liminal moment. The uncertainty of the hour is shown by the fact that Buñuel suggested making two versions of *L'Âge d'or*: one silent, for the many cinemas not yet equipped for sound; the other 'sonore-parlant'.

L'Âge d'or is a real curate's egg, a mishmash of sound effects, talking heads, of silence alleviated by music; the whole sutured along the historical fault-line of the intertitle. Of the ninety-four French films produced in 1930, seventy-six were talkies.[10] Although Buñuel naively believed it would be seen by the masses, his first feature was already technically outmoded, doomed to the cinephile ghetto he despised.

Esplandiu divulges that the pontiffs have landed and that, as feared, they hail from Mallorca. For Dalí and Buñuel, fervent hispanophobes in 1930, Mallorca connoted all that was feudal, God-fearing, reactionary. There is, however, a historical truth embedded in this seemingly private joke. In 1926 Rivera and Mussolini signed a pact to further their geopolitical ambitions in the Mediterranean. In a subsequently leaked secret clause Spain's claims to Tangiers were recognised in return for an Italian base on Mallorca. Mallorquins, then, are metonyms for fascist *Realpolitik*. In July 1936 the Italians would land and the islanders side with Franco.

Putrefaction awaits Péman. He bears the name of another rotter: the Andalusian poet José María Pemán, *bête noire* of the film-makers for his toadying to the Rivera régime. Prévert is left for dead. Cossío hangs back to obsessively whittle a daisy stem while his comrades make off across a landscape as crucifying as any painted in the Holy Land by Burne-Jones. Debussy chirrups ironically. One by one the bandits fall by the wayside: first Esplandiu, Aurenche, Flores. (Miravitlles didn't go to

Catalunya.) Flores' licking of his parched lips comes over as lascivious, announces the orality to come. A general without an army, Ernst scrutinises the coastline for Mallorquins, sees nothing, or something, sinks back dejectedly. We too anxiously scan the chaotic gestalt of light and shade for a sign.

THE THIRD PRISMATIC ARTICULATION

Ernst and his primal horde are never glimpsed again. The bandit sequence is a second red herring. If *Un Chien* had one incongruous prologue, why shouldn't its successor have two? We do now see what Ernst may have seen: a dozen heavily laden dinghies entering a creek. Some of the extras aboard were seasick and landed in soiled suits. The dignitaries who step ashore resemble the mock mourners who chased the hearse in *Entr'acte*, one of the few avant-garde films approved of by the scenarists. Josep Llorens Artigas, the ceramicist who'd become famous for his work with Miró, acts the moustachioed Governor. As the motley crew picks its way across the rugged hinterland it's piquant to think that a 'Club Med' now nestles here. (There was talk in the 70s of putting a commemorative plaque there, but it never happened.) Mallorquins come to pay homage to their countrymen, the host raise their titfers – as do we – to an iconic shot. In the hour that's elapsed since the sentinel espied them the bishops have mouldered into exquisite corpses.

Heymann had a hard time explaining the skeletons and sacerdotal regalia at Spanish Customs. Although Dalí the iconolater said afterwards that the decomposed bishops smacked of simplistic anti-clericalism, at the time he and Buñuel, primed on Péret's ribald iconoclasm, found the gag hilarious. It grew out of an in-joke they'd hatched with Federico García Lorca and Pepín Bello as top-drawer boarders in Madrid's Residencia de Estudiantes. All reactionary ideologues and artists, Péman for instance, were 'putrefacts', rotten to the core, slime, shites. 'Putrefact' and 'Mallorquin' and 'ruling class' are synonyms. The corrupt ecclesiarchs replay 'Finis Gloriae Mundi' – known as 'The Rotting Bishop' to the student farceurs – a grim Baroque painting by Juan Valdés Leal. For Bello the image evoked a visit with Buñuel to a Toledo crypt lined with mummified plague victims, curés included. Buñuel and Dalí, of course, were cocking a snook at the very idea of holy relics, of a fetishism more

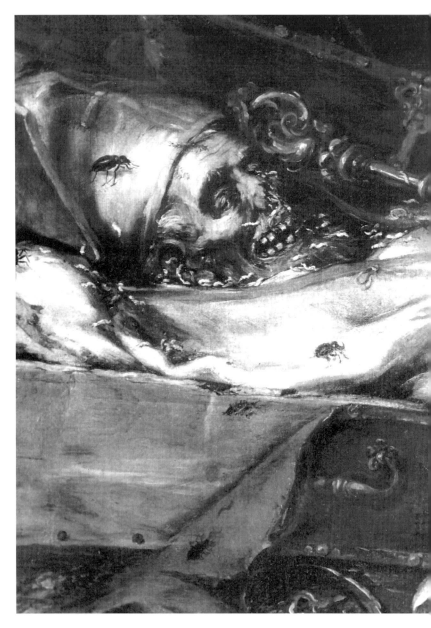

2 0   'The Rotting Bishop'. Detail from Juan Valdés Leal, 'Finis Gloriae Mundi', oil on canvas, 1671–2

unwholesome than a bootlicker's. They weren't to know that one day Generalísimo Franco would never be without the hand of St Teresa of Avila for company, but they might have guessed.

The 'putrefacts' have assembled before a block of granite. The Mozart breaks off. The Governor prepares to speechify, coughs. A shrill cry from the back of the crowd causes heads to turn. Wagner surges. A man (Gaston Modot) and a woman (Lya Lys) are cavorting dementedly in the mud. In the script she manifests 'the greatest tenderness, like that of a mother being caressed by her son'. The images belie this – they're more rumbustious – but the idea will bear bitter fruit.

With his spiv moustache and brilliantined hair – a toupée which the Catalan mistral endangered – Modot was a lantern-jawed double of Adolphe Menjou, the Hollywood actor Dalí and Buñuel lionised, and of Dalí himself. Modot, a fervent hispanophile, friend of Picasso, Cendrars and Mac Orlan, wielded brush and guitar in Montmartre before, in 1910, joining 'Les Pouittes', a team of acrobats who stunted in the scores of 'Onésime' and 'Calino' farces Jean Durand made for Gaumont. Modot wrote gags for these. Between 1919 and 1929 he appeared in three films a year, acting the hard man for Delluc, Fescourt, Dulac. And for Feyder: it was on *Carmen* that he met Buñuel. Modot directed a short in 1928, *La Torture par l'espérance*, based on a Villiers de l'Isle-Adam 'cruel tale'. *L'Âge d'or* was his second sound film, after Clair's *Sous les toits de Paris*. This Communist would become a fixture in Popular Front cinema. Buñuel was suspicious of thespians, preferring actors who'd blindly do his bidding. The forty-three-year-old Modot was a natural, but that didn't stop the director complaining he had too much technique. A willingness to work for half his usual fee, though, cut ice with the penny-pinching Buñuel.

Finding the lead actress – a Louise Brooks type, for preference – proved more problematic. Eight were tested before Buñuel settled on the untried Lya Lys. Her real name was Natalia Lyech, she was Russian and half Modot's age. If Buñuel valued her passive, bovine quality, he was scathing about her inability to follow his direction. Lya knuckled down and by the time the crew returned from Cadaqués she and Luis were lovers. Six months later they'd find themselves in Hollywood, Buñuel twiddling his thumbs, Lys in a bit part in the French-language version of MGM's *Let Us Be Gay*, which starred – Menjou. She stayed on as a contract player and during the 30s appeared in a dozen films, mostly

B-features, but also Lubitsch's *The Merry Widow* (French version, 1934) and Hathaway's *The Lives of a Bengal Lancer* (1935). Bankrupt, Lya retired from films in 1943.

Modot writhes on alone as the couple are separated by the menacing crowd and Lys led away, nuns in attendance. *Carry on Convulsing* suggests itself as an alternative title, since the acting style Buñuel favoured in his first two films is as ham as anything in Gerald Thomas. Desire is represented by heaving bosoms, rolling eyes, bit lips, drool on the chin. 'Considered objectively,' Buñuel would say, 'copulation seems both risible and tragic to me. It's so very like death.'[11] *Abismos de pasión* (1953) is the other movie in the oeuvre that plays it like *L'Âge d'or*. Faced with entering the room by an open door or a closed window Buñuel's rampant Heathcliff will opt for the latter. But then in 1932, when the Brontë film was mooted, such scandalous behaviour was Surrealist common coin; the acme of lyrical being-in-the-world. The first spectacle Buñuel saw on arrival in Paris in 1925 was the Surrealist dustup at the Saint-Pol-Roux banquet. *L'Âge d'or*'s mad mummery also resonates with Breton and Éluard's simulations of schizophrenic utterance in *The Immaculate Conception*. This is Freudian 'acting out' as much as acting.

The *crapule* goes into a brown study, and in 'his voluptuous vision' sees Lys sitting on the john. She has a constipated expression, though we can't see if her drawers are down. The script is revealing here. Although Lys wears an elaborate dress and pearls, our *agents provocateurs* thought to have her garbed in white, very virginal – *the* Virgin, relieving herself. Then the bathroom is empty and the unwound toilet roll burning. The camera might have been shook here for effect. The toilet roll changes walls between shots. (Did Buñuel employ a 'discontinuity girl'?) To the sound of flushing we cut to archive footage of molten lava, bubbling mud. Modot licks his lips. As Dalí said at the time, 'One loves entirely when one is prepared to eat the shit of the beloved.'[12] *Bon appétit*, Salvador!

Two plain-clothes cops hoick Modot from the crud and lead him off towards the laval rocks. Hearing a puppy bark the *enragé* breaks away and gives it a mighty boot. Not so mighty: the whelp had strings attached and was yanked out of shot. Named 'Dalou' – a diminutive of 'chien andalou', but also curiously like 'Dalí' – it became the Buñuel family pet. (When Eric Mottram showed *L'Âge d'or* in Cambridge in 1950 the only complaint came from the RSPCA! Ah, the English.) Modot's indifference tells us that, morally, he's marching to a different drum.

The bantam Governor begins his peroration. The filming was silent and Artigas cracked the crew up with his coarse banter. (A heavenward-gazing curé behind him struggles to keep a straight face.) In the Tobis-Klang sound studio a discourse on collectivising the land was dubbed by Artigas in a strangled French. Phrases like 'raw material' and 'common clay' echo the cloacal mud we've already seen a-bubbling. Did Chaplin crib the idea of garbled speechifying for the statue-unveiling in *City Lights* (1931)? He'd certainly talked to Buñuel in Hollywood by then. But now the obsessive Modot has spotted a beetle. No Fabre, he! Evading the rozzers, he rushes over and, to an audible crunch, flattens it. If I were a critic of the *October* school I'd go on about Bataille's *informe* here. The comic effect comes in part from Modot's choice of opponent: the beetle's not even a scorpion. (Buñuel had asked him to stamp on the dog's head, but the actor refused.) His cowardliness sows the seeds of his future rout. Like all sadists he's a masochist too.

Mendelssohn takes over from Wagner as the deluded debauchee is escorted away. A hod is brought by a mayorial flunkey. The trowel of cement the Governor places atop the granite block is one more turd.

Film and fecality: Keaton in *The Cameraman* (Edward Sedgwick, 1929)

Hollywood silent comedy luxuriated in Bakhtin's 'material bodily lower stratum': shit, piss and spunk to you and me. There are endless examples of victims covered in mud, paint, tar, eggs, feathers. Conversant with Freudian libido theory, Buñuel and Dalí consciously used the oral, anal and phallic as the armature of their movie. Any critic tempted to traduce it psychoanalytically is simply reading what is already written there.

Dalí's theory of 'simulacra', developed during 1929–30 and essentially a rum rewrite of Freud, argued that reality must be understood phenomenologically as the sublimated and endlessly displaced expression, or morphological simulacrum, of unspeakable soma. He classified the returning, repressed signifiers as our old friend putrefaction, plus blood and excrement: an unholy trinity shot through with Thanatos.

In a text which can be dated to June 1930 Dalí wrote: 'We learned long ago to recognise the image of desire behind the simulacra of terror, and even the reawakening of the "ages of gold" behind ignominious scatological simulacra.'[13] Could it be, then, that Salvador baptised the baby? Because *L'Âge d'or* only became *L'Âge d'or* during post-production: *La Bête andalouse*, chosen to suggest continuity with *Un Chien*, is typed on the cover of the shooting script. Buñuel was already unhappy with the title by early May, telling Bello that he favoured *Down with the Constitution!* instead.

The renaming of the film is but one more mystery. Buñuel couldn't remember the how and why of it when Max Aub asked him forty years later. It's been argued that the name alludes to a passage from *Don Quijote* in which that eponymous hero speaks of the mythic Golden Age.[14] Perhaps. But then why not to Otto Rank on the lost paradise of intra-uterine life? Georges Sadoul attacking French capitalism for its ingot-idolatry in *La Révolution surréaliste*? Freud and Ferenczi on the precious metal as surrogate shit? To Lenin and his Bolshevik khazis cast in gold?

I offer the Dalí reference as circumstantial evidence, but finally we can't explain the title. Nor does the title explain the film. It's the old Surrealist gambit: first make the work, then find an anomalous tag, ready-made for preference, to trip its meaning. *The Andalusian Beast* and *Down with the Constitution!* lacked the poetico-philosophical tartness of, say, Breton and Soupault's *The Magnetic Fields* or Breton and

Éluard's *The Immaculate Conception*. Better *The Golden Age*, a found phrase with payload. Bona fide Surrealism.

The turd of cement glues a plaque to the granite block. Presented as a chiselled intertitle, it reads: 'In the Year of Grace 1930, on the site [*les lieux*, which also means 'the loo'] occupied by the remains of four Mallorquins, has been placed the foundation stone of the city of ...'

THE FOURTH PRISMATIC ARTICULATION

We cut to an aerial view of 'Imperial Rome'. Not only has Rome been built in a day, but the trick cut collapses two and a half millenia into one twenty-fourth of a second. (Even dating things from 1506, when the first stone of St Peter's was laid, it's still some four hundred years.) We've been in Italy all along, in Rome-sur-Mer: 'creative geography' with a twist. This articulation, and the next, are the film as Buñuel and Dalí more or less first conceived it.

The jokes reel off in an arch sequence that, using grainy Pathé and Éclair newsreel, pokes fun at the 'city symphonies' of Cavalcanti, Vertov, Ruttmann – and Prévert/Duhamel. Buñuel was debunking himself too: in 1928 he'd written a city symphony script with Ramón Gómez de la Serna called *Caprichos*, but Dalí dissuaded him from making it. A queasy plane-ride takes us over the Roman rooftops. 'The whirl of modern life' means jammed traffic, buckled girders, featureless garden walls, High Mass in the Colosseum. (The contrived banality brings to mind Boiffard's photos in Breton's *Nadja*.) On the Lord's Day a street of houses is dynamited. Do bandits lurk there? The Pope gives a blessing from the balcony of St Peter's. Taped to his cracked window is a scribbled note to a cousin: the Vicar of Christ has renewed the mortgage. As with the Primera–Mussolini 'Mallorca' pact, there's a precise historical allusion here: to the Lateran Treaties of 1929 wherein the Papacy agreed to restrict its temporal sovereignty to the Vatican City in return for lire from the Italian state. The next shot shows a limo in a Roman street. Are Pius XI and cousin aboard, en route to visit the landlord, Mussolini?

A gent leaving a café brushes mud from his jacket. Scripted here, an insert of a hand throwing a glass of wine at the lens. A second bourgeois kicks a violin along the pavement then stamps it. Luis hated

his violin lessons as a kid. These reprises of Modot's earlier outrages are greeted indifferently by the citizenry. A stroller ambles through a park (the Luxembourg Gardens). He balances a stone on his Magrittean bowler hat. It's a gag imaged by Dalí in his painting 'Illumined Pleasures' (1929). The man, who was scripted to have a white beard, walks past a statue of the Catholic writer Bossuet. The bishop too has a stone on his head. This jape is Dalí's only input, they say. Wrongly.

On 29 November 1929 Buñuel arrived in Cadaqués with Noailles's new contract in his pocket and high hopes that he and Dalí would rediscover the harmony of the previous January when their first scenario had flowed from the pen. It didn't happen. In the intervening summer Gala Éluard had come on the scene, salving the hysteria of the twenty-six-year-old virgin and taking his career in hand. But things were not going to plan. Although his first one-man show in Paris had been a success, his new gallery, Goemans, was on the skids. And now Dalí was on a collision course with his father, which would mean goodbye to his allowance. (Bourgeois *señoritos* like Salvador and Luis could expect parental support until well into their thirties.) Buñuel, who'd met Gala in August when in Cadaqués to discuss a second film, was consumed by jealousy, hated her with a passion that overflowed into physical violence. Having got Dalí to break with Lorca – Buñuel was egalitarian in his contempt for gay men and strong women – he was now the supernumary. Despite their bitching the friends blocked out a scenario, which Buñuel took with him to his mother's house in Zaragoza on 6 December.

Buñuel worked on the scenario for a week, on the *découpage* for two. On 29 December he was in Paris, where to his surprise he bumped into Dalí, who'd fled from Catalunya after the family row. They discussed script changes. It was to be their last meeting until *L'Âge d'or* was presented to the Surrealist Group on 30 June. Between 10 January and 8 March painter and muse isolated themselves in Carry-le-Rouet, near Marseille. Later that month they were in Barcelona and in April in Torremolinos. Yet this physical distance doesn't mean Dalí had no more input on the film. It was always understood that Buñuel would actually make *L'Âge d'or*. Although preoccupied with his new 'critical-paranoia' paintings and writings – and with Gala's gynaecological problems – Dalí continued mailing ideas from Carry. And Buñuel duly revised the script to accomodate these often brilliant suggestions.

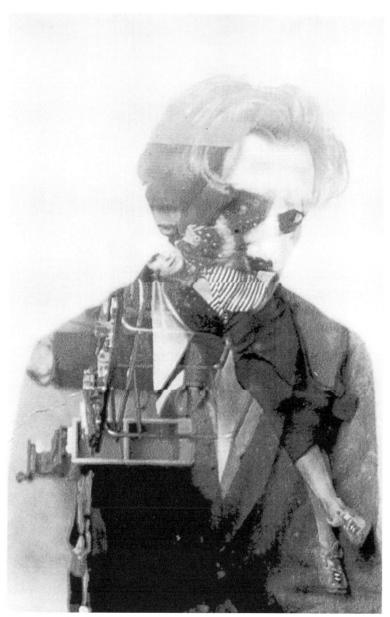

Salvador superimposed on Gala. Photo by Henri Manuel, *c.* 1931
(Fundació Gala – Salvador Dalí)

While they were Surrealists the ambivalent passions subtending their relationship remained buried, but once Buñuel left the group in 1932 they surfaced with a vengeance. The bone of contention was always *L'Âge d'or*, that film which treats of the vagaries of coupledom. When shown in Barcelona in May 1934, for example, the film no longer featured Dalí's name. One could go on totting up the slights committed to print in interview and autobiography during fifty years of self-serving fabulation. Neither testimony is trustworthy, although both protagonists did concur in minimising Dalí's role, albeit for widely different reasons.

In the 60s and 70s Buñuel's first monographers – fideists like Ado Kyrou and Francisco Aranda, intent on claiming their incorruptible subject for the waning Surrealist movement – followed the official line on 'Avida Dollars'. (Dalí worked for free on *L'Âge d'or*!) The film was pure Buñuel; the perfidious dauber had contributed that one gag.[15] This orthodoxy was challenged in 1981 by a critic also formed by Surrealism, Petr Král.[16] Buried for half a century, *L'Âge d'or* could be seen again, and it seemed obvious to an informed viewer like Král that Dalinian imagery suffused the film. (Ask yourself: were hysteria, scatology and onanism the pet subjects of Buñuel, or of Dalí?) Since then the scholarship of Sánchez Vidal in Spain and Bouhours and Schoeller in France has ratified Král's insight.[17] I shall be adding my own pennyworth, putting Salvador back on the screen.

Modot has time-travelled to Rome. Here he is, in shit-stained suit, all basic instinct, still cuffed to, and by, his minders. Passing a hoarding he fixates on a poster of a woman's be-ringed hand reaching for a 'Leda' powder puff. Modot fantasises his lover's ring-finger twitching onanistically: a quivering swatch of hair has replaced the beauty aid and adds to the genital illusion. (His fantasy is generated by wordplay, since *la houppe* means both 'powder puff' and 'curls'.) A choice symbolically functioning object, this, with the arched digit poised like a scorpion's tail to bring *la petite mort*. Modot's delusions persist as a sandwich-man passes with an ad for 'Anitta' nylons. The posters were custom-made by the photographer André Vigneau, whose 1930 was spent making *Balador*, an animated film scripted by Jacques Prévert. Stopping before a bookshop window – the Librairie Espagnole, where Buñuel's fiancée Jeanne Rucar worked – the scoptophile bites his lip at a Man Ray-esque photo of a swooning beauty.

Cued by a shift from Mendelssohn to Wagner, a match cut reveals Lys on her couch, duplicating the swooner's Bernini-like posture. (And echoing the moribund Péman.) In Anitta hose, Leda has been a swan to herself. As the camera dollies back unsteadily we see that her bodice is undone and her ring-finger suspiciously bandaged; another play on words, because *bander* means both 'to bandage' and 'to feel horny'.

The space separating the couple has been transcended; they have come together. If silent comedy was an inspiration for Buñuel, so too was Hollywood *amour fou*: those exorbitant romances depicting lovers who transgress taboos of class, race and creed, time and space, death itself, to realise their passionate dream. Frank Borzage's *Seventh Heaven* (1927) and W. S. Van Dyke's *White Shadows of the South Seas* (1928) are good examples of such 'impossible' rendez-vous of heterosexual desire. When asked in 1935 what for him were model commercial films, Buñuel named *White Shadows* and another Borzage 'mad love' opus, *The River* (1928), movies he'd seen before making *L'Âge d'or*.

We go from Wagner to direct sound. Lys encounters her mother – Germaine Noizet. (This minor stage actress repeated the dowager role in four duff talkies, then went silent.) Seeing her offspring's bandaged

Hollywood *amour fou*: the sewer rat will fall for the guttersnipe in *Seventh Heaven* (Frank Borzage, 1927)

finger curled over the page of a book – the unshot shots of the bishops' digits in their breviaries would have been predictive here – the Marquess makes enquiry. Contemporary audiences hooted when she asks, 'Tu as la main bandée?'. Yes, the lass's finger's been afflicted for a week. Setting aside the double entendre, this begs the question: is Lys's bandage intended to hide an engagement or wedding ring? Is she engaged or already married to Modot? Perhaps Buñuel was unconsciously imaging his own malaise here: his resistance to Jeanne Rucar's wedding plans. (In 1934 they would have to get married.) But the ring imagery was also triggered by the examples in *The Psychopathology of Everyday Life* of parapraxes involving the redoubtable little band of gold. At times *L'Âge d'or* is like a case history you might find in Freud or Krafft-Ebing or Havelock Ellis, the Surrealists' favourite reading during the period of their researches into sexuality (1928–32).

A reaction shot of the mother shows she's wearing a string of pearls and a dress like Lys's on the lavatory. Again, Lya's connection with maternity is subtly made. The masturbation gags keep coming. Is this a highfalutin porno movie? Buñuel's viewing in 1930 included *Sister Vaseline*, a blue film in which a nun, monk and gardener perform. He and

Modot, Lys, Brunius; Heymann, Buñuel and Jeanne Rucar, photographed by Duverger at Billancourt Studios, March 1930 (Fonds Luis Buñuel, Paris)

René Char fantasised about slipping it into a kiddies' matinée. When Lys enquires after her papa we cut to him in his laboratory, vigorously shaking a bottle of liquid plugged by his ring-finger. Like father, like daughter! In a monotone that makes her affirmation doubly strange – Lys is reading her lines – she responds to a question we never hear put that, yes, six musicians, including a Marist, have been hired: 'With these we have enough because six placed near the microphone make more noise than sixty placed ten kilometres away.' The aside pokes fun at the sound revolution. Mother can't abide the 'Surrealist dialogue'. Get moving, the Mallorquins arrive at nine for the concert.

Whatever Kyrou said during auteurism's heyday, Buñuel was no omniscient genius reeling off 'his' films according to an *a priori* interior model. Buñuel never made a secret of the difficulty he had in writing. All his scripts are the work of several hands. *L'Âge d'or*, we know, owes an enormous amount to Dalí. It's most likely indebted to Ernst, Modot, Prévert, Aurenche, Cossío too – not to mention the Surrealist Group, to whom I'll return. Such contributions are difficult to quantify, the wind having whisked away the zest of a thousand inebriated conversations. At this stage in his career Buñuel was free from constraints – thanks to Noailles's backing – but also feeling his way, needing advice and susceptible to influence. His friends among the bohemian Left, rollicking amateurs, provided this. The youth of the team is striking: Buñuel was thirty, Dalí twenty-six; and the two collaborators I want to speak of now – assistant directors Jacques-Bernard Brunius and Claude Heymann – twenty-four and twenty-three.

Buñuel chose them for their experience with sound. In 1929 the well-connected Brunius – he'd worked with Clair and Clair's brother, Henri Chomette, and co-founded important reviews like *Jabiru* (1926) and *La Revue du cinéma* (1929) – made tests for Tobis-Klang of singer Yvette Guilbert. After which he assisted Chomette on *Le Requin*, one of the first 'sonore et parlant' features. Brunius and Buñuel went back to 1927, when Jacques wangled Luis a job as film critic on *Cahiers d'art*. Buñuel duly followed the Brunius line, itself indebted to Desnos. Hollywood and Soviet films were valorised; the formalist French avant-garde denigrated. An inspired dabbler indifferent to his place in history, Brunius would initiate the Prévert brothers into the film biz; work in agit-prop theatre with the 'Groupe Octobre'; make documentaries with Lotar, Vitrac and Desnos; draw close to Breton at the time of 'Contre-Attaque';

act and co-direct for Renoir. Sadly, there's no account of the *L'Âge d'or* experience in his published writings.

Buñuel reckoned Brunius's brilliance, had him pencilled in from the first. Heymann was recruited by early February 1930. Assistant to Renoir on three silents – he also co-scripted *Tire au flanc* (1928) – he'd directed a short, *Vie heureuse*, and a feature, *Deux balles au coeur* (both 1929). More importantly, he was assistant to Robert Florey on the much admired *La Route est belle* (1929), shot at Elstree in a silent and a 'sonore et parlant' version. Heymann was a protégé of Pierre Braunberger, the young tyro who'd set up La Société Studio-Film in 1928 to distribute a new generation of independent film-makers. Cavalcanti, Man Ray, Pierre Prévert and Renoir were on his books. Buñuel too: Braunberger had the foreign rights on *Un Chien*. When sound arrived he bought Billancourt Studios and, still only twenty-five, went into production with Roger Richebé. Much of *L'Âge d'or* was shot at Billancourt. Other Braunberger hands would help Buñuel out: Georges Van Parys (music), Marc Allégret (casting) and Roger Woog (budget).

Entering a barn of a bedroom Lys is unfazed to find a vast Normandy cow on the bed. Her imperturbability gives point to the

3 4   Ernest Bourbon in *Onésime and the Camel* (Jean Durand/Gaumont, c. 1913)

theme of Roman anomie. The upper class don't give a fig for the 'animal' lower orders. (The bandits were licked in advance, then!) A cow-bell tinkles. The recumbent cow reworks the putrescent donkeys on the piano in *Un Chien*, but lacks its richness. Although there's a 1928 Dalí oil called 'The Spectral Cow', the idea *per se* may have originated with Modot, who'd appeared in an 'Onésime' farce in which a donkey is seen abed. (Richard Abel has identified this as the 1913 *Onésime et son âne*.) The adolescent Buñuel was a big Onésime fan.

We've seen how wordplay generates imagery. *Vache* (cow) could refer to Lys, or her mother; or to the cops (*vaches*) holding Modot; or to *amour vache* (the rough stuff). The docile beast is shooed from the room. Sitting at her dressing-table Lys automatically polishes her nails with a 'miraculous nail-buff' – the title of a 1927 Buñuel poem. Her bandage has disappeared: a planted lapsus. She's *débandée*, both 'unbandaged' and 'detumescent'.

Barking joins the cow-bell, bringing Pavlov to mind. We cross-cut to Modot and his *vaches* being yapped at by another mutt. This time, hand over heart, he looks tenderly and tearfully at the dog, paralleling his distant lover's gestures. Her own crossed hands reveal the bandage back in place. There's an inimical religiosity to these images. As Lys gazes into her magic mirror front-projected clouds scud across it. Another Magrittean touch; reminding us that, with Dalí, Magritte was the influential new star in the Surrealist firmament. Ruffling her hair, the whistling wind from the mirror joins the barking and tinkling. It explicitly evokes Breton's definition of *le merveilleux* as a zephyr at the temples. This supernatural meeting is as good as things will get. Abjection awaits: more tears and endless bungling.

The sounds are indicative of Lys's mental state. Generally speaking, however, such transcendental synaesthesia is avoided. Although often combined with music, sound effects tend to be mimetic and synchronised. Likewise dialogue, 'Surrealist' or otherwise, is usually delivered in a sound vacuum. Buñuel was proceeding tentatively in the new medium. Was his use of sound as innovatory as some have suggested? To answer that definitively we'd need to know more about the seventy-five other French talkies released in 1930.

We dissolve to Modot and escort. Raving on, he insults a passer-by (Brunius) with 'Filthy swine!' (*sale vache!*) Only now does the enragé acknowledge the cops. He'll show them who's who, and produces an impressive document. In flashback, and to Mozart, the Minister of the Interior hands Modot, identified in the script as the Honorable Mr X, his portfolio: he's a member of the International Relief Committee. (Another in-joke, since Buñuel got to Paris as an apprentice official of the International Institute of Intellectual Cooperation). Like a schoolgirl racing through her catechism, Lord Muck sings out that he's responsible for the lives of countless children, women and old folk. We see how seriously he takes his mission when, to the amazement of the now-deferent policemen, he takes time from hailing a taxi to kick a blind war veteran to the ground. A fulsome provocation, this, given that the Anciens Combattants were the most powerful political lobby in the land. In 1927 the right wing of this anti-democratic movement took the name 'Les Croix de feu'. With the ascension after 1929 of the retired colonel François de la Roque the 'Crosses of Fire' became a paramilitary force organised along Mussolinian lines. They would play a major part in the fascist riots of February 1934 which ushered in the *Front Populaire*.

THE FIFTH PRISMATIC ARTICULATION

To strains of Schubert, an intertitle announces that the Marquises of X will be receiving guests in their magnificent property outside Rome. We recognise the Marquis as Lys's self-abusing father. The flies stuck to his face signify he's a 'putrefact'. Bonaventura Ibáñez, the Spanish character actor, asked Buñuel for double pay to suffer this indignity. The 'X' could mean 'Christian', as in 'Xmas'. The Marquises, their daughter and Modot are all Xs: one big happy family?

Were Buñuel's satirical barbs intended to snag his patrons? Was he biting the hand that fed him? Their abundant correspondence – the Vicomtes wintered at their Hyères property in Provence for most of the filming – would suggest not. Within their respective worlds – aristocratic salon and lumpen-bourgeois café – the parties were assiduously non-conformist, and valued each other as such. Buñuel hid nothing of the film from his 'dear friends'. The more outrageous the better, was the agreed plan.

The Noailles were no strangers to avant-garde movie production. Jacques Manuel, Man Ray and Pierre Chenal all received commissions in 1929. (Chenal would supply the film stock for *L'Âge d'or*.) In 1930 it was the turn of Buñuel and Jean Cocteau. Christian Zervos of *Cahiers d'art* and Georges-Henri Rivière, co-editor of *Documents*, presented Buñuel to the Noailles sometime after the one-off screening of *Un Chien* at the Studio des Ursulines on 6 June 1929. During July the couple promoted the film, showing it to the cultured *beau monde* of Paris in their private cinema on the Place des États-Unis. Buñuel had arrived. It was Marie-Laure, the power behind the throne and a poet and painter in her own right, who urged Charles to fund a sound sequel to *Un Chien*: the film was to be her birthday present. Buñuel was delighted, but refused a proposed collaboration with the 'Catholic' Stravinsky. Producer and director struck a bargain: 75 per cent of the take to the Vicomte, until his investment was paid off, after which all profits to Buñuel. Both patron and protégé expected their film to be a commercial success.

It's during this fifth chapter that *L'Âge d'or* most closely imitates Hollywood in its no-frills editing and functional photogenia. Aside from his filmography, which extends from 1919 to 1933, we know little about

Albert Duverger. Buñuel had assisted on two features shot by this jobbing cameraman – Epstein's *Mauprat* (1926) and Etiévant's *La Sirène des Tropiques* (1927) – before asking him to film first *Un Chien* and then *L'Âge d'or*. Duverger photographed several Benito Perojo films and most likely spoke Spanish, an asset given Buñuel's imperfect French.

Although he played fast and loose with its conventions, Luis was a Hollywood man at heart. In 1929–30 his role models were Fred Niblo, James Cruze, Mal St Clair, Luther Reed; with, at the top of the tree, Borzage, Lubitsch, Stroheim, Keaton. Buñuel never ceased working within – and across – the dominant

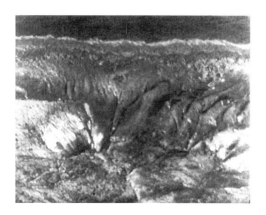

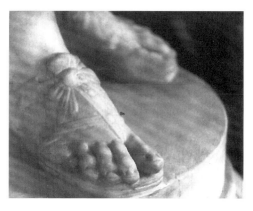

The lower orders

Hollywood codes. At the start and finish of his career such radical conservatism was his way of disavowing the 'art' film. In between times it was a formal obligation, given the subaltern status of Spanish and Mexican cinema. Apropos of *L'Âge d'or* Heymann remarked that 'such a destructive work could assume its true value only if it was structured precisely within the framework of a "bourgeois" film.'[18] The analogue in painting would be Magritte, who planted his depth charges within a ready-made, academic realism.

Newcomers to *L'Âge d'or* even now find it chaotic; and yet the average shot length, leaving aside the tacked-on epilogue, is 5.5 seconds. This figure tallies with contemporary Hollywood and French silents. Buñuel cuts no quicker than Epstein or Tod Browning, say. Average shot lengths don't, however, say what a shot contains. Here it's a question of quality, not quantity; each shot being violently overdetermined. The cutting is stately even, compared to *Un Chien* where it's twice as fast, every three seconds.

A Rolls brakes, a footman lifts out an ostensory, a woman's stockinged leg steps on to the running board. A fleeting juxtaposition that functions symbolically, at least for me. I believe the woman is Valentine Penrose, the Surrealist poet and future biographer of Erzsébet Báthory. It was when the ostensory – a piece of altar furniture used to display the consecrated host at Catholic Mass – appeared that the fascists started laying about. In Surrealist parlance the Holy Sacrament was the 'Holy Excrement'. Buñuel and Dalí invented many a poem title about the host: with moustache and prick; coming out of a nightingale's arse, saluting; combating ants. Dalí drew the last in the souvenir programme.

Inside the sumptuous salon the Marquises of X welcome the diminutive founder of Rome and his tall, horsey wife. (She's played by a doctor relative of the Surrealist artist Valentine Hugo.) Mussolini had his admirers in the French Establishment. It was only after the Nazis' massive election victory in September 1930 that Hitler would displace him. The interiors are by Pierre Schildknecht – aka Schild – a Russian émigré who'd designed *Un Chien*. Buñuel knew him from *La Sirène des Tropiques*. True to Dalí's prognosis that paranoia makes the world go round, the Italian ambassador in Paris lodged an official complaint at this perceived guying of his monarchs. In their tract 'The *L'Âge d'or* Affair' (January 1931), the Surrealists juxtaposed a still of Artigas and Mme Hugo with a snapshot of Victor Emanuel III and his Queen, captioned

'Their Italian Majesties, who murder revolutionary workers, such as they are in sad reality.' Objection sustained.

Buñuel called on friends and acquaintances to play, gratis, the guests. You got a part if you owned a tux or party frock. Some were Buñuel's ex-fellow students at Epstein's Académie de Cinéma, White Russians who extraed for Albatros Films. Other faces belong to Roland Penrose, Simone Cottance, Joan Castanyer, Marie-Berthe Ernst, Domingo Pruna. Penrose, Ernst's chum, would help organise the 1936 International Surrealist Exhibition in London, give up Valentine for Lee Miller, set up the ICA Brunius's eccentric sister, Simone Cottance, was part of the cinephile circle that included Jean Mitry, Jean-George Auriol, Paul Gilson. It was Simone who alerted Jacques, who alerted Breton, to that 'Surrealist Manifesto of Cinema', *Sherlock Jr*. Castanyer, a hard-drinking Catalan painter with an anarchist past, would design sets for Renoir, come up with the idea for *Le Crime de Monsieur Lange* (1935) and produce Republican newsreels in war-torn Barcelona. (His superior there was Jaume Miravitlles.) Marie-Berthe, Jean Aurenche's sister, was Max's wife and the inspiration for one of his collage-novels. Since she'd just appeared in Gilson's short *Crime, accident ou suicide?*, Buñuel tested her for the Lya Lys role. A film journalist and translator of Ramón's scenarios for *La Revue du cinéma*, Pruna worked with Cavalcanti, then directed the first Catalan talkie *El Cafè de la Marina* (1933). In 1936 he'd assist on two of Buñuel's Filmófono productions.

Faced with the disruptive presence of the plebs the Mallorquins don't bat an eyelid. Like the scorpion, they have an immense instinct for self-preservation. The tumbrils of the Terror are history, so the ghastly horse and cart that trundles across the room with its carousing Cloggies is politely ignored. (This was one of the gags Buñuel wrote in summer 1929, when he began planning a follow-up to *Un Chien*.) A similar fate awaits the maid – Caridad de Laberdesque, a Montparnasse barfly and heroinomane who'd recently distinguished herself in a Surrealist raid on the 'Maldoror' nightclub – torched by an exploding kitchen range. Yet Buñuel nuances any 'us and them' tub-thumping by showing that the élite servants are just as indifferent to their colleague's fate as the toffs. The French Communist Party (PCF), cleaving to its 'class against class' line, cannot have been best pleased, comrade. The higher-up lackeys even unconsciously mimic the body language of their paymasters. Manifesting the latent meaning of gesture was how Buñuel 'irrationalised' Hollywood melodrama. When the edgy Lys strokes her unbandaged ring-finger a dissolve superimposes a butler feverishly fingering a smeared decanter. 'You're *all* wankers!' seems to be the message.

Speaking of *L'Âge d'or* forty years later Buñuel said: 'It's a clear, resolute film, without mystery. Zilch. Very Surrealist of course, but there's no mystery to it. My ideas are clearly visible. Not mine, the ideas of the Surrealist Group are perfectly visible.'[19] Are we to take this statement literally? To conclude that Buñuel had the Surrealists vet his script? It's probable that at the twice-daily café meetings there was at least some discussion of the movie-to-be.

Un Chien was Buñuel and Dalí's passport into Surrealism. The Wall Street Crash had done wonders for the intellectual allure of the Comintern – and thrown the Surrealist movement into crisis, with Breton purging all those who declined to follow the PCF line. After seeing friends like Jacques Prévert, Desnos and Boiffard go over to the opposition – Georges Bataille – Buñuel and Dalí signed a declaration of faith in both the *Second Manifesto* and the Revolution. Becoming a Surrealist was something of a religious conversion for Buñuel. His reply to the December 1929 'Inquiry on Love', for instance, is of the utmost orthodoxy. Too perverse by half, Dalí wasn't even asked. Yet as the Stalinist convictions of Buñuel grew, inexorably driving a wedge between him and Breton, the latter came to prize the Catalan Wunderkind's tenacious iconoclasm, in the short term at least.

The Mark II Surrealists needed a good scandal to boost their morale. Were *L'Âge d'or* to be a riot, it would give them greater visibility and more clout, not least with the Party. An elaborate forty-eight-page booklet was prepared for the November launch at Studio 28. Written by Breton, Crevel, Éluard, Aragon and Thirion, the 'Manifesto of the Surrealists Concerning *L'Âge d'or*' reveals not only how they wanted the film to be read, but also how, trapped in ideology, they only incompletely understood it.[20] How far the burlesque brio of Buñuel's film is from this ponderous, triumphalist rehash of Hegel, Freud, Sorel and Lenin! And how blind the authors to the fact that love *fails* to conquer all in *L'Âge d'or*. When Breton affirmed in 1937 that the movie exalted love as he envisaged it, the irony and unwitting candour of his words passed him by.

I'd hazard a guess that, generally speaking, the 'social' jokes are Buñuel's, the 'sexual' ones Dalí's. The two combine in the gamekeeper sequence, one of the movie's most violent and perverse. It was shot last.

Manuel Ángeles Ortiz, a Picasso imitator where painting and women were concerned, and a member of Luis's mock 'Order of Toledo', plays the gamekeeper. (That's him sitting by the dormant cow in the still you all know.) Cretinous of countenance, the son of Buñuel's concièrge acted the boy. In the script the victim was a daughter. Too little time, too much rain, and the increasing hostility of the aghast owners of the Montmorency location perhaps made Buñuel improvise and change the victim's sex. It's tempting, however, to see Dalí's influence once again, and Dalí's Oedipal obsession with William Tell. Hadn't the working title of *Un Chien* been *The Marist in the Crossbow*? This Tell does not miss. 'Hijo de puta' (little bastard!) we lip-read as Ortiz bags the boy. (The gag replays Picabia's gunning down of Jean Borlin in *Entr'acte*.) The father's over-reaction to his son's mischief – think of Salvador's problems with Dalí Sr – is cross-cut with the under-reaction of the aristos to prole violence. Sadism is ubiquitous, part of everyday life; its differing expression merely a question of breeding. Ortiz was inducted at the last minute. Had the director earmarked the role for himself? He liked shooting guns and playing the bruiser. This could backfire: as a homage to Buñuel's belligerence Jean Painlevé invited him to a screening of *Dr Claoué* (1930). Buñuel nearly puked at the documentary images of the pioneer plastic surgeon at work.

Waiting for Modot, Lys scratches her itchy finger. Seen from behind, he arrives in Magrittean overcoat and bowler, trailing a dress, a duplicate of the one Lys is wearing. Tossed on to an armchair it lands, miraculously, in a sitting position. (Reverse motion; a trick inherited by the avant-garde of Clair, Richter and Buñuel from primitive comedy.) The image reworks the cyclist's bisexual drag laid on the bed by his lover in *Un Chien*. Half-fetish, half-relic, the cocktail dress also rejigs the pontificalia on the rocks.

Dalí's symbolically functioning 'Aphrodisiac Jacket' (1936) condenses elements from the slapped Marquess scene: the glasses attached to the dinner jacket contain liqueur and a dead fly

A dissolve puts meat on the bone: Lys filling out that frock, the very incarnation of Modot's stubborn will to delusion. The remainder of this key chapter articulates, in a *mise en scène* that owes something to Lubitsch and to Stroheim, a great, a grand deception. This is the nub of the film, the gist of the jest. All the cocked snooks and blind alleys lead here. Modot and Lys want to screw but succeed in screwing up. We've been warned they would. Phantasy made flesh remains phantasy, traumatically so.

Modot's expression on entering is, the script says, 'a mixture of love and deceit'. If this is so – and for me the acting doesn't put it across – then all that follows is ironising sham, a double bluff. What price his lip-biting, his show of 'unbridled lubricity' as his eyes meet hers across the crowded room? (Aside from announcing a libertine theme à la Sade, that is.) Beelining for Lya, Gaston is stopped by her mother. The Marquess greets him warmly, implying 'that it wasn't long before, a few hours ago perhaps, when she last saw the person'. The plot between the 'Xs' thickens. Don't laugh, but I did think to propose to you earlier that Modot and Lys are not just husband and wife but also brother and sister.

The drinks trolley, with its freshly polished decanter, hoves into view and the 'deceitful' guest hints he'd murder a martini. (A 'buñueloni', natch.) The Noblesse obliges, spills the proffered beverage on Modot's hand – not, as scripted, on his trouser flies – and is slapped by that hand. Shades of the Surrealist admonition of Mme Rachilde at the Saint-Pol-Roux banquet; double pay for Noizet. All hell breaks loose. A slapped Marquess has more worth than a slaughtered child. The snarling Marquis has to be held back: no flies on him now! Modot defends his outrageous action with the same insouciance as Ortiz. Lys, the object of his unwavering gaze, is exalted. He bows to the serried fists and leaves, sad sack dress in tow. She dutifully consoles her snivelling mum.

Seconds later the churl is back, gesticulating to Lys to go outside. It's as if Modot has no memory of the slap, the script says. The amnesiac Basil Fawlty crosses the salon, ignoring the glaring toffs, who are, anyway, too polite to eject him a second time. The show must go on; the orchestra is tuning up. Its white-bearded conductor chats to a manikin Marist Brother, incongruous cig in one hand, violin in the other. He's scripted as a pianist, an unpacking of the famous portmanteau image in *Un Chien* of two Marists roped to two pianos.

With its topiary hedges, cypresses and classical statuary Schildknecht's set replicated, it's said, the family garden in Calanda, the one where Margarita Buñuel was almost stung by a scorpion. The Böcklinesque gloom of the place also evokes Dalí's angst-ridden 'William Tell' (1930), a painting which quotes the pianos and rotting donkeys of *Un Chien*.

The smooth cross-cutting shuttles between the lovers' lapsi and the orchestra recital. Jean Epstein had used recordings of Wagner, Schubert, Mozart, Beethoven to sonorise screenings of *Mauprat*. Buñuel borrowed the idea from him for *Un Chien*. In the case of *L'Âge d'or* the discs were re-recorded on to the soundtrack. Brunius kept these 78s until he died. They are now in the collection of the English Surrealist John Lyle.

Tristan and Isolde in the garden. Etching by Franz Stassen, *c*. 1900

'They're playing our song,' Modot and Lys might well say, for each time they meet it's to a theme from *Tristan und Isolde*; usually 'The Death of Isolde'. While Buñuel described himself as 'an incorrigible Wagnerian' in 1930,[21] his choice of this particular opus is interesting. (He'd used it in *Un Chien* and would do so in *Abismos de pasión*.) For Denis de Rougemont the twelfth-century romance of Tristan and Iseult established the very notion of love in the Occident. In short, what the lovers love is less each other than the fact of loving. Each loves the other not as they really are but as a mirroring of their personal desire for oneness. Driven by nostalgic narcissism, the lovers' passion can subsist only by placing obstacles in its path. The absolute obstacle, and thus passion's true object, is death itself. Rougemont takes Wagner to be the first to have uncovered the latent meaning of this archetype.[22]

Earlier I said the acting is ham; 'operatic' is another way of putting it. As Gaston and Lya go down the garden path towards their apotheosis, the Wagner we see being played, or mimed, doesn't just ironically counterpoint the action – as soundtrack – it determines it as diegesis. This was a constant in early sound cinema: one often *sees* sound being emitted, from a radio, a violin, a tap shoe.

McTeague bites Trina's fingers in *Greed*

We cross-cut from the aristos taking their seats on the terrace – one concert-goer's menses could stain her dress, suggested Dalí – to the over-anxious lovers tumbling from their seats in the garden. A statue of Venus, the Roman goddess of love, presides over their farcical and prolonged coitus interruptus. Modot, his eyes glazed, takes Lys's fingers into his mouth – her ring is visible – she his. Buñuel reworked Dalí's proposal – stronger than the razored eye in *Un Chien*, the painter said – to have the man frenziedly bite and rip off the woman's fingernail. She'd scream and then proceed as if nothing had happened. It's possible Buñuel was glossing the scene in Stroheim's *Greed* (1923) of McTeague biting Trina's fingers so she'll tell where her gold is. (Thereafter Trina has her fingers bandaged.) The oral sadism is belied by the ecstatic smile on the faces of Modot and Lys, and the joyous reciprocity of their cannibalistic gesture. But sadism there is, as we see his hand caressing her cheek – minus the fingers. A mis-matching insert substitutes an amputated hand with its obscenely phallic thumb. The suggestion is that Modot desires to be – or to go on being – castrated; and that Lys is happy to oblige. In imagination, that is, for in the ensuing shots his fingers are intact.

Dalí had big ideas for the love scene. He'd found, he said, a way of realising Buñuel's 'long-standing dream of [showing a] cunt in cinema'.[23] The amorous woman should incline her head so her lips were 'north-south', so to speak, and in big close-up. Then a dissolve, to superpose the labia of a depilated vagina. Or alternatively the superimposition of a *décolleté* framed by a feather boa – 'pubic hair' – with the lips gradually seceding to a heaving bosom. Dalí was practising 'critical paranoia' here, a methodology inspired by the dissolves of film language. His idea revamped the images in *Un Chien* when breasts metamorphosed into buttocks, a hairy armpit into a sea urchin.

The conductor onanistically taps his baton – *une baguette*, which also means 'prick' – on his rostrum. Wagner varooms and the startled lovers bang heads. Modot is about to kiss Lys when his attention is grabbed by Venus's foot. He signals her to wait. The insert of the marble foot marks an inhibition. It could be a synecdoche for Roman authority or a dead mother; an index of Modot's propensity for automatically associating ideas – hand and foot – or a gag about a nutter who'd rather screw a statue than a woman.

Although they'd sworn allegiance to Breton, the scenarists undoubtedly knew Bataille's essay 'The Big Toe'.[24] Buñuel for one privately maintained cordial relations with Bataille's circle. It's tempting to read the scene as a coda to the Bataille, especially since the gunge so dear to the 'excremental philosopher' is also the lovers' elective element. The source, however, is just as likely to be Dalí's own essay 'The Liberation of the Fingers', which precedes Bataille's by six months, and predicts it.[25] In any case Modot's attention is drawn to the whole foot: this is simply an allusion to fetishism.

To keep us on our toes Buñuel slips in an anomalous gag of three Marists racing in fast motion across a footbridge. A fourth hoves into view, the runt violinist, and he stops to stare in panic at the fixated lovers – or us – before scurrying off. A private joke again, Buñuel's answer to a riddle set in his 1927 poem 'The Rainbow and the Poultice': 'How many Marists fit on a footbridge? / Four or five?'[26] It's an image Renoir would purloin in *Une Partie de campagne* (1936) when one of the scuttling seminarists is, strange to tell, Georges Bataille.

Modot claps hand to brow. Venus has broken the spell. 'All you with lead in the head, melt it to make Surrealist gold.'[27] Like Bossuet's statue, like the stroller in the park, he's had a weight on his mind. But no more. The lovers twirl, fall to the ground. Let's fuck!

We cut to the Marist's masturbatory fiddle-work; a hex. There's a crunch on the gravel. A majordomo approaches: the Minister of the Interior wants Modot on the phone. The polymorphous pervert stumps off in a fury, hankie hanging 'symptomatically' from his breast pocket like the shirt that poked out of the bandit's flies.

In frustration Lys turns to Venus's big toe and gives it the full Mae West treatment, sucking lustily. 'Ah! the young girls who lift their dress / and wank off in the bushes / or in the museums / behind the plaster Apollos' (Péret).[28] Lya's a recidivist of the simulacrum, an oral sublimator. Her Oedipal desire is suggested by a cut to the statue's head and then to the Marquis, seated beside his still sniffling wife. Papa's head leans at the same angle as Venus's. The Wagner ends.

The Minister – the obscure actor Evardou – toys with a pistol as he upbraids Modot. There's been an uprising, many deaths, the ingrate's to blame, the Minister has been compromised. The disaster was scripted to have an exhausted man emptying baskets full of children's shoes on to a heap, and a sobbing mother pressing her daughter's dress to her breast: Stroheimian touches that resonate grotesquely with Modot's fetishism. Time and budget were against Buñuel and, as with the scorpions, our *bricoleur* resorted to archive footage. We see a Spartakist mob charge across a square and poor families fleeing a city threatened by flowing lava. (The men wear 'bandit' hats; the lava we've already seen.) The lumpens come from Henry King's *The White Sister* (1923), a Papist tearjerker starring Lilian Gish, shot in Italy. 'You disturb me just for that!' Modot bawls. 'The devil take 'em, your brats!' and he rips the phone off the wall.

Bang! The Minister's receiver dangles beside blood, gun, shoes. The camera pans up from this Langian shot to frame his stocking-footed corpse blasted and plastered to the ceiling, then pans down to blackness. An improvement, this gag, on the planned insert of blood dripping into shot from on high and a horizontal pan to the cadaver on the floor. The Wagner resumes.

So too the 'hymeneal rites'. The fellatrix simmers. Kneeling between her open legs Modot, paralysed by inhibition, goes off the boil. He imagines married life, sees his paramour age thirty years, become a Roman matron. Or perhaps he takes Lys for a double of his own mother. The voice-over dialogue is strictly Darby and Joan. Bedroom talk, but unerotic: 'Where's the light switch?' 'At the foot of the bed.' What price mad love? Cross-cut with sawing violins and swaying conductor, the lovers sentimentally embrace. Lys dozes. Dalí's suggestions for the noise of pissing in a pot and creaking bed-springs were rejected, but lip-smacking we hear.

The dialogue – it's Dalí's – is dreamy. But whose dream? They're making love; *amour vache* perhaps. This is how it should be! The vibrato Wagner steers them to orgasm. Lys is wide-awake, rapt. 'I've been waiting for you so long,' she ejaculates. 'What joy to have murdered our children!' The matron's a Messalina at heart. The gamekeeper's infanticide was predictive, the Minister's accusation justified. Paul Éluard's voice speaks for Modot, whose face is lacerated, left eye sanguine, lips horribly rouged. 'Mon amour, mon amour,' enunciated the way poets do: 'Mon ameuur.' (I'd conjecture that Lys's lines are spoken by Éluard's lover, Nusch.) We're reminded of Fabre on insect courtship; on the sadism of the female and masochism of the male during copulation. Love can make you lose your head.

The 'lead in the skull' gags proliferate. Cut to the conductor jettisoning baton, burying head in hands, sobbing. The orchestra halts; the audience mutters. The conductor lurches off into the gloaming,

'Are you cold?', from *Le Surréalisme au service de la Révolution*, 1 July 1930. The bishop is Marval; the girl Suzanne Christy, first choice for the Lya Lys role. Photographer unknown, but probably Duverger

footfall crunching. Lys dozes as the neuralgic spectre approaches. Modot's unbloodied gaze is heavenward, ecstatic. Roused, aroused, she bites her fingers, rushes to the bearded patriarch, hugs and kisses him on the lips. Lys baulked at this kiss. Buñuel understood. He too found the actor Duchange repulsive: a mineralised old fool, he said.

Modot is aghast at this uninhibited avowal of incestuous desire. Rising angrily to intervene, he cracks his noggin on a hanging basket. In the script he has a flash of the bishops on the rocks, though not here. The ecstatic drums of Calanda roll from now until the end. *His* hands clapped to his forehead, a sobbing cuckold retraces the conductor's footsteps.

The bandits, the Mallorquins, Lys and, hitherto, Modot were in thrall to the simulacra. Now the headbanger has come to his senses. Love? You can shove it! With malice aforethought he enters the traitress's bedroom. As he passes the camera we observe a button poking over his trouser-fly: another planted parapraxis; Dalí's doing. Also his, the (unused) idea of a piano waltz to accompany Modot's revolt against the deathly Symbolic Order. The snarling enragé falls upon the cow's bed and eviscerates a pillow. Hands full of duvet – signs of onanistic impotence, as Chaplin and Langdon knew – he rampages, his frenzy driven by the Calanda tattoo. (Isn't drumming displaced wanking?) Caesar/Mussolini's bust falls from his grasp. Modot hefts an incongruous plough, its beam a mighty dick. He opens the window. We cut to an exterior, low-angle view. In rapid succession a blazing fir, bishop, crosier and plough are defenestrated, a rite that reprises the scene in *Un Chien* where Batcheff's fetish gear is thrown out the window. A shot from Modot's point of view shows the fallout thirty feet below. The bishop picks himself up and hightails it. A fifth object emerges, a giraffe.

Deducing that these phallic objects connote family, religion, work and nature – or love? – doesn't diminish the mythic lustiness of Modot's *potlatch*. Here he's more Buñuel's double than Dalí's. Buñuel seems to have believed de-sublimation was possible. Dalí was less sure. He liked playing with his toys. Buñuel wanted to break them.

The plough throws us back to the Governor's speech, to his cult of the soil, of manure. The crosier and bishop – he's played by Marval, the film's production manager and one of the burdensome Marists in *Un Chien* – present no problem for the understanding. The flaming fir and giraffe are more heteroclite. As to the latter, Heymann tried to hire a stuffed specimen, but when the suppliers learned it was to be set alight they said no. This explains the model shot and toy giraffe. Was the Xmas tree torched in its place? Whatever, these things challenge our reason. In May 1933 Buñuel's 'Une Girafe' appeared in the last issue of *Le Surréalisme au service de la Révolution*. In this Péret pastiche, written at the end of 1931, the beast is a Trojan horse of Oedipal simulacra. Cue the giraffes in Little Hans's phantasies; the burning ones in Dalí's pictures.

In slow motion the dinky giraffe plummets down a plaster precipice into the waves. More 'creative geography'. Buñuel imagined freeze-framing on the splash. Next, an insert of a hand releasing feathers into the void. The camera pans down, though barely: the feathers are already up to the ledge. A jump-cut, then, to hint that purging takes time, forever. We leave Gaston to his Sisyphean self-abuse, since a sudden intertitle brings 'the fifth prismatic articulation' to a end.

A SIXTH VESICULAR JOINT, THE POISON SAC

The intertitle announces another narrative swerve. What follows is, we read, synchronous with the falling plumes and involves 'the survivors of Selliny Castle'. For those in the know – a handful in 1930 – said survivors fix the moment in the early 1700s: they're characters from Sade's *The 120 Days of Sodom*. The intertitle is one more mendacious mismatch. The epilogue is Buñuel's own work. Can he get his hero out of a hole?

The feathers dissolve into snow and the camera pans up a white scarp to frame a distant fortress. (Another model shot.) Its occupants are described in a long rolling intertitle which, in symmetry with the Fabre, quotes but doesn't credit book or writer. What grabs the attention is the profound misogyny of the four atheist libertines, for whom 'the life of a woman – what am I saying, of a woman? – of all the women who inhabit the surface of the globe, is as insignificant as the destruction of a fly'. A provocation, yes, but the simile does ratify the psychoanalytic insight that insects are linked to castration anxiety in the masculine psyche. (Vide Modot's vainglorious stamping of the beetle.)

The lurid pen portrait primes us for the first gag. We're told to expect the arch-sodomite, another degenerate aristo, the Duke de

Blangis. The castle door opens and out steps Jesus. Twenty years ago this blasphemy seemed archaic. Now that religious fundamentalism has returned to plague the world it resonates again. Contrary to myth, Lionel Salem, who acts 'The Turk', as Buñuel called him, was not a Christ specialist. In fifteen screen performances he played the part twice, first in *L'Agonie de Jérusalem* (Julien Duvivier, 1926), then in *L'Âge d'or*.

Dazzled by the studio snow, Blangis blesses the barrenness, crosses the mini-drawbridge and ascends a shamelessly cardboard incline. (I've visited Sade's recently restored château in the Vaucluse. It looks oddly like this set.) Three wasted libertines follow, dressed in feathered tricorns, ruffles, cloaks. We don't know who acted them; the second, though, is a dead ringer for Robert Desnos. The third uses a crutch, echoing the bandit Cossío. Libertines, Mallorquin bishops and Marists come in fours. Libertines, Mallorquin bishops and bandits are very tired.

Buñuel's joke blends *The 120 Days* with the Marquis's *Dialogue Between a Priest and a Dying Man*. 'Return to your senses, preacher,' the priest is cajoled, 'your Jesus is no better than Mohammed, Mohammed no better than Moses, and the three of them combined no better than Confucius.'[29] Buñuel considered doing the Blangis/Christ gag thrice over with the ruling class roués named as Président Curval, Financier Durcet and the Bishop of K, and costumed respectively as Confucius, Mohammed and 'a priest of the 16th century'. (Luther?) After lauding the 'Freudo-Sadism' of *L'Âge d'or*, the great Sade scholar Maurice Heine, an ultra-leftist sympathiser with Surrealism, chided Buñuel for stepping back from this quadruple blasphemy, a criticism that still pained him forty years later.

Buñuel, whose own accounts of discovering Sade are confused, probably first read him sometime late in 1929, when Roland Tual, an ex-Surrealist who would become manager of Billancourt Studios, lent him *The 120 Days*. Written in 1785 on a scroll ten metres long, eleven centimetres wide – the better for hiding in his cell – Sade last saw his masterpiece when transferred from the Bastille just before its fall. Believed lost in the looting, he spent the rest of his life rewriting it. His 'Rosebud' had, though, survived and in 1904 Eugène Dühren (Iwan Bloch) published a strictly limited but badly garbled edition in Berlin. This was the version Buñuel read. 'In Sade I discovered a world of extraordinary subversion encompassing everything from insects to the customs of human society, sex, theology. In short, he really dazzled

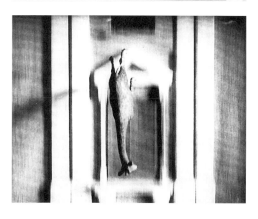

Imaginary compensation

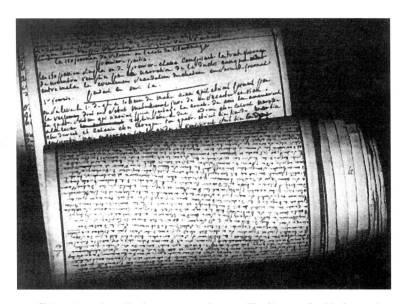

me.'[30] Simply to handle the auratic volume – Tual's copy had belonged to Proust – was doubtless an initiation of its own into the forbidden.

In January 1929 the scroll came to auction and Noailles, a collector of Sade manuscripts – Marie-Laure was distantly related to the writer – bought it. *The 120 Days* would appear after 1931 in Heine's impeccable edition. Thanks to his scholarly labours between 1926 and 1935, Sade was very present in the minds of the Surrealists, the cherry in a fierce cocktail of Lenin, Hegel and Freud. As well as demonstrating his Surrealist orthodoxy in invoking *The 120 Days*, Buñuel was paying the patrons a pretty compliment. In August 1930 Marie-Laure gave him Sade's *The Misfortunes of Virtue*, hot from the press, with a chummy dedication: 'For Luis Buñuel, this little family souvenir.' Four months later *L'Âge d'or* blew up in all their faces. Sade and Buñuel would be united in one thing: a lifetime spent reworking an Ur-text disappeared by history; scroll and reel.

Selliny – Silling in the book, which makes you wonder how well Buñuel knew it – has a further surprise in store. Clutching her blood-stained breast, a young girl in underclothes collapses across the threshold. (Hardly young: a heavily pan-caked Caridad de Laberdesque in her second role.) Arms open in Christian charity, Blangis crosses the

Manuscript scroll of *The 120 days of Sodom,* owned by Charles de Noailles.
Photo by Boiffard

drawbridge, raises her up. She places her head against his chest, as Lys had done with the bearded conductor. The Saviour helps her back inside. In the script it's the Bishop of K who shows mercy. The atmosphere on set, said Heymann, was decidely uneasy during the shooting of this scene. The camera stays on the closed door. The drums mute a little. A scream is heard: another echo of Lya when she mud-bathed with Modot. The door opens and Blangis exits – minus beard. (The last time I saw the film in public nobody seemed to notice this; or if they did no one laughed.) Gazing piously heavenward, the depilated assassin glides past the camera while his phallocrat confrères shuffle off to inspect the damage.

The drums give way to a jaunty paso doble – it was Wagner crossed with a tango in *Un Chien* – and we dissolve to a leaning cross covered in snow. The six female scalps hanging from it sashay obscenely in the swirling wind; one more symbolically functioning object, another holy relic, a last gag linking hair and symptom. The Christian symptom, the image says, is genocidal hatred of women. The same could be said of the vaginophobic pornology of Sade: did Buñuel twig this when he equated Christ and Blangis? Eight seconds later *L'Âge d'or* is done, spent, its final burst of Nietzschean laughter doing little to resolve the ambivalence of Buñuel (and Dalí) towards femellitude. The problematic of desire can be exercised, not exorcised. Desire is impossible, desire is.

The theme of the film is frustration. The form of the film mirrors its theme. There's no resolution, only deferral, qualification, blurring. False starts and false endings. Pessimism writ large. A belt in the teeth. The only way out is to buckle the belt. Fabre's rock cedes to the hard place of Sade, shimmering chiaroscuro day to bleakest snowy night. We began with humanity effaced. We end with effaced humanity.

Buñuel needn't have worried. History was about to foreclose his first feature, terminate the interminable for him. The *L'Âge d'or* lights stayed on the marquee for twelve days. Then came fifty years of near-invisibility – and myth-making.

A shape-shifter, Buñuel, a trickster who liked to hit and run. Study his movements in the four months after completing his film and you find that, aside from one aborted séance for the Surrealists, he avoided each and every screening. Fatigue? Disdain? Modesty? Cowardice? Dalí for one was miffed at having to face the music alone. Already hounded from Catalunya, he stood to be ejected from France as an undesirable alien. Buñuel didn't take that chance: he ran before he hit.

Both patron and protégé expected their film to be widely shown. The only overtures, however, came from Jean Mauclaire: he wanted *L'Âge d'or* for Studio 28, the 337-seater repertory theatre in Montmartre where *Un Chien* had been shown for the last twelve weeks of 1929 as the support, with three other shorts, for a Donald Crisp thriller, *The Cop*. Mauclaire was also an independent producer: in 1929 he financed *La Perle* (d'Arche and Hugnet), *Harmonies de Paris* (Lucie Derain), *Nuits électriques* (Eugène Deslaw). As an inducement this medical student turned cinephile undertook to sonorise his auditorium – a costly commitment – and to wangle the film past the censors. In private Noailles and Buñuel were disparaging of Mauclaire's avant-gardisme, but once they'd encountered the indifference of the few boulevard Odéons equipped for sound, and interested only in blockbuster Hollywood musicals and melodramas, they changed their tune. During September 1930 Buñuel interrupted his *pourparlers* with Laudy Lawrence, the MGM talent scout in Paris, to co-ordinate the Studio 28 opening. And to ready *L'Âge d'or* for presentation to the Commission de Censure.

After 1919 all films were viewed by a commission appointed by the Ministry of Public Education and Fine Arts and given a visa – or not. On 18 February 1928 the Centre-Right government of Poincaré passed a decree designed to bring the provinces into line with Paris; to prevent

films being censored again by local zealots. This liberalising measure was married to protectionism: foreign movies were acceptable as long as the exporting country agreed to import in kind. It goes without saying that the moral yardstick of the censors was ultra-conservative and inexact. Formally the power of the thirty-two commissioners devolved 50–50 to government functionaries and to laymen from inside and outside the film industry. In practice only two censors examined

Jean Chiappe, Prefect of Police. His sacking brought fascist mobs out on to Paris streets in February 1934. Buñuel would exact a sweet revenge against the inventor of the zebra crossing in *The Diary of a Chambermaid* (1964)

material, one from Public Education, the other from the Ministry of the Interior. Censorship was secretive – and political. 'Bolshevik' films were particularly targeted, either heavily cut or banned outright. Paul Ginisty, liberal president of the Commission in 1930, admitted that the Ministry of the Interior had nobbled Pudovkin's *Mother*. The man who had the Minister's ear was Jean Chiappe, Prefect of Police in Paris and a rabid anti-Communist. 'Jean-Fesse' (Jean Arse), as the PCF's paper *L'Humanité* called him, was a buff: Gance screen-tested him for the role of Napoléon. Protector of the extreme Right, Chiappe hated the fellow-travelling Surrealists. Eisenstein fared no better. The police let him lecture at the Sorbonne in February 1930, but *The General Line* couldn't be screened.

On 29 September Mauclaire presented a fanciful synopsis of *L'Âge d'or*, along with a list of the intertitles, to the commission. As he'd anticipated, the censors didn't bother to view the film, asked for a change to one intertitle, and granted it a visa on 1 October. Buñuel considered Mauclaire's résumé a comic masterpiece, which indeed it is:

> This film, which begins with an extended and searching documentary on the life and manners of the scorpion, plus several fine sequences of the great outdoors and of rugged rocks, passes directly to the misadventures of one of those excitable types unhinged by modern life. Believing himself mandated to do good,
>
> he takes it into his excited and sick mind not to do so; on the contrary, through his improbable attitude he contrives to upset a fashionable soirée. A very fine number by a classical orchestra of fifty musicians is presented during the course of this soirée. Then, victim of a banal accident which further excites his thoughts and his fragmentary visions, and which the author has not ceased indicting

Jean Mauclaire, the director of Studio 28 who defended the embattled film against the wishes of the director and producer

throughout the film, he disappears following a series of incomprehensible acts. The film redeems its difficult and unfathomable subject through a consistent and well-rendered sense of humour, which gives this obviously fanciful work an imprimatur of smiling philosophy.[31]

Despite Buñuel's absence – he was visiting his mother in Zaragoza, prior to taking up his MGM contract – Noailles did his bit, screening *L'Âge d'or* for the salon crowd in his private cinema and then, on 22 October, at a gala preview at Braunberger's Cinéma du Panthéon. The glitterati loved it. Dalí was delighted. The minority of aristocrats left without a word. Some of them would squeal to the papers. The Establishment was closing ranks. On 9 November – the day Buñuel dined with Chaplin in Hollywood – Cocteau's byline appeared in *Le Figaro*, defending their patrons against an irate press.

L'Âge d'or opened at Studio 28 on 28 November, on a bill with Abric and Gorel's *Paris Bestiaux*, a documentary which predicts Franju's *Le Sang des bêtes* (1948); Leonid Moguy's *Au village*, a Soviet kolkhoz comedy; and a cartoon (probably Disney or Fleischer). Copies of the gold-covered brochure containing the Surrealists' manifesto were available, as were their revues and books. An exhibition of paintings by Dalí, Arp, Ernst, Miró, Man Ray and Tanguy was mounted in the foyer. The producers stayed away from the first night – Charles had a symptomatic ear infection – but Salvador was there. The new sound system malfunctioned. Look on the bright side, Dalí told Noailles, at least there was no scandal.

The Vicomte, by now in Hyères, had five days to wait for the dreaded news. On 3 December fifty demonstrators from Les Jeunesses patriotes, an offshoot of La Ligue des Patriotes, and La Ligue anti-juive, allied to L'Action française, laid waste to Studio 28, throwing ink at the screen, letting off smoke bombs and roughing up spectators, before trashing paintings and books. Eleven arrests were made, including one Ernest Sade, aged eighteen, in all likelihood a student: the universities were a recruiting ground for the Jeunesses patriotes. The session continued with paper masking the inkstain. For a week the cinema was heavily policed by both gendarmes and PCF militants. On 5 December the Prefecture demanded that the scenes of the bishops be cut; Mauclaire complied. On the 7th a municipal councillor, Gaston Le Provost de

Launay, watched the matinée before addressing an outraged missive to Chiappe, duly leaked to *Le Figaro*. On the 9th the censors told Mauclaire that, following a protest by Mussolini's ambassador, he must re-present the film on the 11th. That evening two agents from Chiappe's General Intelligence Department spectated. Reading like Mass-Observation, their report asserts that the bandits killed the bishops; that the diploma Modot presents to his minders is 'masonic'; that Artigas's medals are Belgian. Interestingly, Studio 28 was only two-thirds full, and the audience a mixed bunch, both Rightists and Leftists. On the 10th Mauclaire read in the evening paper that screenings had been discontinued: he was told officially only later that night. On the 11th the Commission de Censure lied that since their first viewing (*sic*) certain 'pornographic' scenes had been added. On 12 December Chiappe impounded the two prints in Mauclaire's possession. (A third remained in the hands of the Librairie Espagnole.) *L'Âge d'or*'s visa was withdrawn. Thirteen thousand souls at most had seen it; probably half that.

Le Figaro and *L'Ami du Peuple* spearheaded the moral panic: Judeo-Bolshevik devil-worshipping masonic wogs did this, they hollered. The anti-Semitic attacks distressed the Noailles: Marie-Laure

'Christian illiteracy': the ink-stained screen at Studio 28, 3 December 1930
(Fundació Gala – Salvador Dalí)

was the daughter of a Jewish banker. Both papers belonged to François Coty, the perfume king, and financier of L'Action française and Les Croix de feu. *L'Ami* did unconsciously comprehend *L'Âge d'or*, dubbing it *L'Âge d'ordure* (The Age of Excrement). *L'Humanité* counterattacked, accusing Chiappe and Coty of being 'at the service of fascism and the bourgeoisie'. The totalitarian battle-lines were drawn. They would swell during the decade.

Telegrams and letters sped back and forth between Hollywood, Hyères and Paris. 'I take full responsibility,' said Buñuel. 'Keep me out of the papers,' Noailles, who'd already been blackballed from his club, pleaded. (The story that the Princesse de Poix entreated the Pope not to excommunicate her son Charles is, it seems, just that.) Jeanne Rucar and Juan Vicéns of the Librairie Espagnole liaised with director and producer, rescuing the negative and facilitating a one-off screening in London arranged by Nancy Cunard. Pulling strings in the new government of Théodore Steeg, Mauclaire doggedly fought on alone against the ban. Buñuel, pushed by an anguished Vicomte, manoeuvred to stop him, citing a clause that revoked their contract if screenings were once interrupted. Noailles cannot have welcomed the noisy anticensorship activities of Radical-Socialist deputies Aimé Berthod and Gaston Bergery, and André Berthon, a Communist. Chiappe stood firm: even censored, *L'Âge d'or* endangered public order.

The Surrealists, meanwhile, milked their media notoriety, publishing a tract, 'The *L'Âge d'or* Affair'.[32] A questionnaire composed by Aragon and Éluard appeared alongside press cuttings and photos of the wrecked cinema. The questions followed the PCF line: 'Isn't the use of provocation to legitimate subsequent intervention by the police a sign of fascisation?' The tract spoke apocalyptically of 'the coming war, especially that against the USSR'. Dalí was among the sixteen signatories.

By 24 January 1931 the negative was back in Noailles's hands. His other grand production of 1930, Cocteau's *La Vie d'un poète*, had also run up against the censors. After this baptism of fire Charles would renounce film-making and tend to his roses.

Studio 28 reopened in February with a substitute programme of 'the least bad sound and talking films made till now', kicking off with *The Hound of the Baskervilles* (Richard Oswald, 1929). Mauclaire went bankrupt soon after and fled to China. At the end of the same month

GRANDES CARRIÈRES

PRÉFECTURE DE POLICE

D^{on}　　　　B^{au}

Procès-Verbal du *11 décembre 1930*

Aff^{re} c/ *Mauclaire (Jean)*

Scellé N° *Un*

Les bobines du film "L'Âge d'or" contenues dans six boîtes en carton portant des étiquettes avec le titre primitif du film, "La bête Andalouse", faites au "Studio 28".

Il s'agirait d'une copie de secours qui n'a jamais été projetée.

Police seal on the seized film (Fundació Gala – Salvador Dalí)

Buñuel announced his early departure from MGM. His stay in Hollywood had been even less productive than Eisenstein's. Arriving penniless in Paris in early April, he borrowed money from Jeanne and journeyed to Zaragoza to see mater. There he witnessed the tumultuous founding of the Second Republic. By 27 April he was back in Paris, sounding out the possibility of dubbing work for Paramount. Were Buñuel and Dalí among the unnamed 'foreign comrades' who signed the Surrealist tract, 'Torch it!', vaunting the holocaust that, after 10 May, consumed five hundred Spanish churches and convents? In mid-May he and Charles de Noailles met face to face for the first time in over six months. They set to renting copies of *L'Âge d'or* to cine-clubs in Berlin and Buenos Aires. Or better yet, selling: Noailles wanted to recoup his investment. Luis was skint.

On 22 November, and for the first time, the director personally presented his film at an invitation-only screening in Madrid. Given the recent anti-clerical unrest there was no question of *L'Âge d'or* being shown publicly in Spain. The Librairie Espagnole print had the odd

The film is linked to the Depression, which would hit France late in 1931. Caption: 'L'Âge d'or … it's like prosperity … it can't last forever!' From *L'Ami du Peuple*, 15 December 1930

outing, always in a film club context: Marseille in February 1932; Brussels in May. Buñuel described how two Paris showings had passed off without incident: 'A few claps at the end and the public exited extremely depressed. No protests.'[33] The director too was dejected: 'I find myself very far from the spirit of *L'Âge d'or*,' he told Noailles.[34]

Or, put another way, from Surrealism, since Buñuel's affiliation to the movement began wavering as a new split developed around the figure of Louis Aragon. The so-called 'Aragon Affair' has been recounted many times in the history books. Briefly: Aragon's position within Surrealism had been ambiguous ever since, under pressure from the Communists, he'd co-signed, with Sadoul, a letter at a revolutionary writers' congress in Kharkov denouncing Trotsky, Freud and Breton. In Paris Aragon and Sadoul partially retracted their testimony. Early in 1931, along with Pierre Unik and Maxime Alexandre, they joined the PCF. (For Aragon and Unik, their second time: they'd been members in 1927.) Buñuel, it appears, did likewise. In November the police seized a revue containing Aragon's agit-prop poem 'Red Front'. In January 1932 the poet was indicted for 'demoralisation of the army and the nation'. The Surrealists came to his defence with a tract, 'The Aragon Affair'. By March some three hundred intellectuals – including Buñuel and Dalí – had manifested their solidarity. Breton cited their names in a subsequent polemic, 'Misery of Poetry', in which he attacked both the 'pro-fascist' justice of the bourgeois state *and* the *proletkult* philistinism of the PCF: the Communists had denounced Dalí's 'pornographic and counter-revolutionary' text 'Rêverie'. Aragon parted company with the Surrealists the moment he disavowed the 'Misery' tract in the pages of *L'Humanité*. Buñuel's sympathies lay with Aragon and the PCF. The old rancour against Dalí resurfaced: 'he [Dalí] now represents the Surrealist extreme right', Buñuel wrote tendentiously to Noailles on 17 March.[35] Sadoul, Unik and Alexandre followed Aragon out of Surrealism. So did Buñuel: on 6 May he sent a letter of demission to Breton saying he couldn't stay in a group 'whose aims had become incompatible with those of the Party'.[36]

It was during these ructions that, on the advice of Pierre Braunberger, Buñuel decided to present a reworked *L'Âge d'or* to the censors. The new twenty-minute version would be called *In the Icy Water of Egoistical Calculation*, a phrase drawn from *The Communist Manifesto*. Noailles was agreeble – 'a most elegant solution' – and conceded all profits to Buñuel and Braunberger. He asked only that the sequences of the ostensory, of 'the personage in white', and the hirsute cross be dropped. On hearing of the project Breton lamented that the director had given in to his PCF friends and agreed to bowdlerise his film.

The only eye witness account we have of this phantom work is Edmond T. Gréville's. While at Billancourt cutting his fourth feature, *Plaisirs de Paris* (1932), the director chanced upon a can containing a roll of celluloid labelled *Les Eaux glacées du calcul égoïste*: 'I put it on the moviola straightaway. It was a compilation of certain scenes the Mexican director had rejected from *Un Chien andalou* and his next film. It constituted a sort of digest of Surrealist cinema.'[37] Gréville's recall is at odds with the film-maker's. Buñuel spoke at the time of avoiding trouble by excising the sequence of Modot booting the blind man, which suggests that *In the Icy Water* was indeed an expurgation. An unnecessary precaution, because on 23 September the Commission de Censure refused it a visa. Buñuel fulminated against Chiappe and fascist arbitrariness. But to no avail: *L'Âge d'or* was dead and buried.

Well, not quite. There always were pirate copies in existence – seven, Buñuel reckoned in 1974 – and very occasionally these would be

screened, with or without Noailles's official blessing. The artist Patrick Hughes recalls first 'seeing' *L'Âge d'or* in a London pub in 1961, but through the eyes of George Melly. Melly's shot-by-shot description was so vivid that when Hughes actually viewed the movie years later it seemed flat by comparison. Not everybody was so well informed about this legendary work: in the mid-70s *Time Out* advertised a rare showing of *Large Door*. In-between times the Vicomte kept faith with his Father Confessor – Buñuel too, in a sense, because he respected his old patron's

Although annotated 'Madrid 1932', this is more likely Buñuel before or after the film's one-off screening at the Palacio de la Prensa, 22 November 1931

religious convictions – waiting until the last year of his life to divest himself of a cross he'd borne for fifty years. In 1980 the distribution rights were auctioned in France, Britain and the States. Since then we've been able to see *L'Âge d'or* without any to-do. Today there must be thousands of video dupes in existence, given that the movie is considered benign enough to go on the telly. It is no longer a *film maudit*. Neither is it wholly domesticated. A holy relic can always move the faithful fetishist. Caught like an arachnid in amber, in the amber glow of its own golden age, Buñuel's second film remains an object of fascination, of perturbation, of *productive* nostalgia. The dagger of the projector beam may yet bear some poison.

Luis Stylites, atop his pillar in Zaragoza, 1997

NOTES

· ·

1 Salvador Dalí, *The Secret Life of Salvador Dalí* (New York: Dial Press, 1942), p. 304.
2 Gianni Rondolino, *L'occhio tagliato. Documenti del cinema dadaista e surrealista* (Turin: Martano, 1972), pp. 222–51. I shall often refer to the shooting script as published in Rondolino; without, for brevity's sake, giving page references.
3 J. H. Fabre, *Souvenirs d'un entomologiste* (Paris: Club des Libraires de France, 1955), p. 251.
4 J. H. Fabre, *Social Life in the Insect World* (Harmondsworth: Penguin, 1937), p. 94.
5 The identification of Miravitlles – and Esplandiu – is conjectural. We know they appeared, but putting a face to a name is something else altogether.
6 Salvador Dalí, *Le Mythe tragique de L'Angélus de Millet* (Paris: Jean-Jacques Pauvert, 1963).
7 Salvador Dalí, 'Objets surréalistes', *Le Surréalisme au service de la Révolution* no. 3, Paris, December 1931, pp. 16–17.
8 Translated in Paul Hammond, (ed.), *The Shadow and its Shadow: Surrealist Writing on the Cinema* (Edinburgh: Polygon, 1991), pp. 55–9.
9 Luis Buñuel, 'Del plano fotogénico', *La Gaceta literaria* no. 7, Madrid, 1 April 1927, p. 6. Reprinted in Buñuel, *Obra literaria* (Zaragoza: Ediciones de Heraldo de Aragón, 1982).
10 I've relied here on Richard Abel, *French Cinema: The First Wave, 1915–1929* (New Jersey: Princeton University Press, 1984), pp. 59–65.
11 Tomás Pérez Turrent and José de la Colina (eds), *Buñuel por Buñuel* (Madrid: Plot, 1993), p. 115.
12 Salvador Dalí, *La Femme visible* (Paris: Éditions Surréalistes, 1930), p. 67.
13 Ibid., p. 18
14 Agustín Sánchez Vidal, 'De *L'Âge d'or* à *La Ruée vers l'or*', in Jean-Michel Bouhours and Nathalie Schoeller (eds), *L'Âge d'or. Correspondance Luis Buñuel – Charles de Noailles. Lettres et documents (1929–1976)* (Paris: Les Cahiers du Musée national d'art moderne. Hors-série/Archives, 1993), p. 19.

15 Ado Kyrou, *Luis Buñuel* (Paris: Seghers, 1962). Translated as *Luis Buñuel: An Introduction* (New York: Simon & Schuster, 1963); J. Francisco Aranda, *Luis Buñuel: Biografía crítica* (Barcelona: Lumen, 1975).
16 Petr Král, '*L'Âge d'or* aujourd 'hui', *Positif* no. 247, Paris, October 1981, pp. 44–50.
17 Agustín Sánchez Vidal, *Buñuel, Lorca, Dalí: El enigma sin fin* (Barcelona: Planeta, 1988); Sanchéz Vidal (1994), 'The Andalusian Beasts', in Michael Raeburn (ed.), *Salvador Dalí: The Early Years* (London and New York: Thames & Hudson, 1994); Bouhours and Schoeller (eds), *L'Âge d'or. Correspondance.*
18 Claude Heymann, 'Sur le tournage de *L'Âge d'or*', *Jeune Cinéma* no. 134, Paris, April–May 1981, pp. 6–11.
19 Max Aub (ed.), *Conversaciones con Buñuel. Seguidas de 45 entrevistas con familiares, amigos y colaboradores del cineasta aragonés* (Madrid: Aguilar, 1985), p. 134.
20 Translated in Hammond (ed.), *The Shadow and its Shadow*, pp. 195–203.
21 Aranda, *Luis Buñuel*, p. 139.
22 Denis de Rougemont, *Love in the Western World* (New York: Pantheon, 1956), pp. 227–31.
23 Sánchez Vidal, *Buñuel, Lorca, Dalí*, p. 240; Bouhours and Schoeller (eds), *L'Âge d'or. Correspondance*, p. 53. Undated letter, Dalí to Buñuel (between 10 January and 8 March 1930).
24 Alan Stoekl (ed.), *Visions of Excess: Selected Writings of Georges Bataille, 1927–1939* (Manchester: Manchester University Press, 1985), pp. 20–3. 'Le gros orteil' appeared in *Documents* no. 6, Paris, November 1929. Allen S. Weiss, 'Between the Sign of the Scorpion and the Sign of the Cross', in his *Aesthetics of Excess* (Albany: State University of New York Press, 1989), is an excellent reading of *L'Âge d'or* from a Batailleanperspective.
25 Raeburn (ed.), *Salvador Dalí*, p. 228. Dalí's 'L'alliberament dels dits' appeared in *L'Amic de les Arts* no. 31, Sitges, 31 March 1929.
26 Buñuel, *Obra literaria*, p. 137.
27 José Pierre (ed.), *Tracts surréalistes et déclarations collectives, Tome 1 (1922/1939)*

(Paris: Eric Losfeld, 1980), p. 33. A Surrealist
papillon (sticker) from 1924–5.
28 Benjamin Péret, *Les Rouilles encagées*
(Paris: Eric Losfeld, 1970), p. 35.
29 D. A. F. de Sade, *Justine*, *Philosophy in the
Bedroom and Other Writings* (New York:
Grove Press, 1965), p. 172.
30 Pérez Turrent and Colina, *Buñuel por
Buñuel*, p. 29.
31 Bouhours and Schoeller (eds), *L'Âge d'or.
Correspondance*, pp. 80–1. I've retained
Mauclaire's clumsy syntax.
32 Pierre (ed.), *Tracts surréalistes*, pp. 188–93.

33 Bouhours and Schoeller (eds), *L'Âge d'or.
Correspondance*, p. 155. Buñuel letter to
Noailles, 10 May 1932.
34 Ibid., p. 153. Buñuel to Noailles, 23 March
1932.
35 Ibid., p. 150.
36 Mark Polizzotti, *Revolution of the Mind:
The Life of André Breton* (London:
Bloomsbury, 1995), p. 375.
37 Edmond T. Gréville, *Trente-cinq ans dans
la jungle du cinéma* (Arles: Institut Lumière/
Actes Sud, 1995), pp. 116–17.

CREDITS

. . . .

L'Âge d'or

France
1930
Produced by
The Vicomtes Charles and
Marie-Laure de Noailles
Budget
715,500 francs (approx.
£5,800 in 1930)
First private screening
30 June 1930
Venue
The viewing theatre of the
Noailles mansion in the
Place des États-Unis, Paris
16
**First public screening to
an invited audience**
22 October 1930
Venue
Le Panthéon Cinema, Paris
**French commercial
release**
28 November 1930
Venue
Studio 28, Paris
**Date of banning by the
Prefecture of Police**
10 December 1930
**First UK screening to an
invited audience**
2 January 1931
Venue
The Gaumont Company
Theatre, London
**First UK commercial
release**
January 1980
Venue
The Institute of
Contemporary Arts,
London
Director
Luis Buñuel
Scenario
Luis Buñuel and Salvador
Dalí
Shooting script
Luis Buñuel

Assistant directors
Jacques-Bernard Brunius
and Claude Heymann
Editor
Luis Buñuel
Production manager
Marval
Production assistant
Jeanne Rucar
Budget supervision
Roger Woog
Photography
Albert Duverger
Set designer
Pierre Schildknecht
Assistant set designer
Serge Pimenoff
Studio stage manager
Jean Gastaldi
Sound engineer
Dr Peter-Paul Brauer
Sound montage
Kracht
Sound system
Tobis-Klang
**Musical extracts on
disc, chosen by Buñuel**
Mendelssohn's *Hebrides
Overture* and *Italian
Symphony*; Mozart's *Ave
verum corpus*; Beethoven's
5th Symphony; Debussy's 'La
Mer est plus belle'; Wagner's
'Forest Murmurs' from
Siegfried; 'Prelude to Act
One' and 'The Death of
Isolde' from *Tristan und
Isolde*; 'Gallito' (paso doble);
the Good Friday Drums of
Calanda (Aragón), played by
twelve drummers of the
Republican Guard;
occasional music by
Georges Van Parys
Laboratory
G M Film, Auteuil

Film
Agfa and Kodak 35mm
panchromatic black and
white
Film supplier
Pierre Chenal
Stills photography
Albert Duverger
Stills printer
E Cornille
Posters seen in the film
André Vigneau
Archive footage
The White Sister (Henry
King/Metro Pictures,
1923); *Le Scorpion
languedocien* (André Bayard
or J. Javault/Éclair, 1912);
newsreel footage from
Actualités Pathé and Éclair-
Journal
Shot at
Studios de Billancourt (silent
sequences: 3-26 March 1930);
Studios de la Tobis, Épinay-
sur-Seine (sound sequences:
31 March-1 April).
On location in Cap de
Creus, Catalunya (5-9
April); Montmorency
(Seine-et-Oise) and the
16th arrondissement of Paris
(19-24 May)
63 minutes
1715 metres; 5615 feet

Gaston Modot
The man, *the Honorable
Mr X*
Lya Lys
The woman, *daughter of the
Marquises of X*
Germaine Noizet
The Marquess of X
Bonaventura Ibáñez
The Marquis of X
Josep Llorens Artigas
The governor

Mme Hugo
The governor's wife
Manuel Ángeles Ortiz
The gamekeeper
Duchange
The orchestra conductor
Lionel Salem
The Duc de Blangis/Jesus Christ
Caridad de Laberdesque
The screaming maid/the blood-stained maiden
Max Ernst
The leader of the bandits
Pierre Prévert
Péman, the bandit abed
Francisco G Cossío
The lame bandit
Pedro Flores, Joaquín Roca, Juan Esplandiu, Jean Aurenche and Jaume Miravitlles
The other bandits
Marval
The defenestrated bishop
Valentine Penrose
Woman in car with ostensory

Marie-Berthe Ernst, Roland Penrose, Domingo Pruna, Simone Cottance, Joan Castanyer, Joaquín Peinado, Raymond de Sarka and unknown extras from Films Albatros
Guests at the Marquis of X's concert
Jacques-Bernard Brunius
Passer-by in the street
Claude Heymann, Marie-Berthe Ernst, Juan Ramón Masoliver, Jaime Otero, friends from Barcelona and residents of Cadaqués
Mallorquin crowd-members
Evardou
The Minister of the Interior
B. Aliange and Gilbert
The policemen
Denic and Pereirra
The carters

The son of the concièrge of 7, rue du Laos, Paris 15
The gamekeeper's son
Josep Albert, Firmo Maula, Enriquet Maula, Mario Coll
The bishops on the rocks
Jean-Paul Dreyfus
One of the Marists on the footbridge
Paul Éluard
Voice-over during the garden lovemaking scene
'Dalou'
The maltreated dog

The above credits – slightly revised and expanded – draw on Bouhours and Schoeller (eds), *L'Âge d'or: Correspondance* and David, *¿Buñuel!*: essential sources.

Credits checked by Markku Salmi.

BIBLIOGRAPHY

Abel, Richard, *French Cinema: The First Wave, 1915–1929* (New Jersey: Princeton University Press, 1984).

Aranda, J. Francisco, *Luis Buñuel. Biografía crítica* (Barcelona: Lumen, 1975). The English translation (London: Secker & Warburg, 1975) omits some of Buñuel's critical writing and interviews.

Aub, Max (ed.), *Conversaciones con Buñuel. Seguidas de 45 entrevistas con familiares, amigos y colaboradores del cineasta aragonés* (Madrid: Aguilar, 1985). The perhaps more accessible French translation lacks, alas, 39 of the 45 interviews.

Bouhours, Jean-Michel and Schoeller, Nathalie (eds), *L'Âge d'or. Correspondance Luis Buñuel – Charles de Noailles. Lettres et documents (1929–1976)*, (Paris: Les Cahiers du Musée national d'art moderne. Hors-série/ Archives, 1993).

Buñuel, Luis, 'Del plano fotogénico', *La Gaceta literaria* no. 7, Madrid, 1 April 1927, p. 6. Reprinted in Buñuel, *Obra literaria*.

———— *Obra literaria* (Zaragoza: Ediciones de Heraldo de Aragón, 1982). Introduction and notes by Agustín Sánchez Vidal.

———— *Mon dernier soupir* (Paris: Editions Robert Laffont, 1982). Translated as *My Last Breath: The Autobiography of Luis Buñuel* (London: Jonathan Cape, 1984). Nothing alerts the English reader to the fact that the text is edited and rearranged.

Dalí, Salvador, *La Femme visible* (Paris: Éditions Surréalistes, 1930).

———— 'Objets surréalistes', *Le Surréalisme au service de la Révolution* no. 3, Paris, December 1931, pp. 16–17.

———— *Babaouo, scénario inédit; précédé d'un Abrégé d'une histoire critique du cinéma; et suivi de Guillaume Tell, ballet portugais* (Paris: Éditions des Cahiers libres, 1932).

———— *The Secret Life of Salvador Dalí* (New York: Dial Press, 1942).

———— *Le Mythe tragique de L'Angélus de Millet* (Paris: Jean-Jacques Pauvert, 1963). The text dates from 1933.

David, Yasha, *¿Buñuel! Auge des Jahrhundets* (Bonn: Kunst und Ausstellungshalle der Bundesrepublik Deutschland, 1994). The Spanish version, *¿Buñuel! La mirada del siglo*, is slightly revised (Madrid: Museo Nacional Centro de Arte Reina Sofia, 1996).

Fabre, J. H., *Social Life in the Insect World* (Harmondsworth: Penguin, 1937).

———— *Souvenirs d'un entomologiste* (Paris: Club des Libraires de France, 1955).

Gréville, Edmond T., *Trente-cinq ans dans la jungle du cinéma* (Arles: Institut Lumière/ Actes Sud, 1995). The text dates from c. 1965.

Hammond, Paul (ed.), *The Shadow and its Shadow: Surrealist Writing on the Cinema* (Edinburgh: Polygon, 1991).

Heymann, Claude, 'Sur le tournage de L'Âge d'or', *Jeune Cinéma* no. 134, Paris, April–May 1981, pp. 6–11. An interview with Lucien Logette in 1978.

Král, Petr, 'L'Âge d'or aujourd'hui', *Positif* no. 247, Paris, October 1981, pp. 44–50.

Kyrou, Ado, *Luis Buñuel* (Paris: Seghers, 1962). Translated as *Luis Buñuel: An Introduction* (New York: Simon & Schuster, 1963).

Péret, Benjamin, *Les Rouilles encagées* (Paris: Eric Losfeld, 1970). A text dating from 1928.

Pérez Turrent, Tomás and Colina, José de la (eds), *Buñuel por Buñuel* (Madrid: Plot, 1993).

Pierre, José (ed.), *Tracts surréalistes et déclarations collectives. Tome 1 (1922/1939)* (Paris: Eric Losfeld, 1980).

Polizzotti, Mark, *Revolution of the Mind: The Life of André Breton* (London: Bloomsbury, 1995).

Raeburn, Michael (ed.), *Salvador Dalí: The Early Years* (London and New York: Thames & Hudson, 1994).

Rondolino, Gianni, *L'occhio tagliato. Documenti del cinema dadaista e surrealista* (Turin: Martano, 1972).

Rougemont, Denis de, *Love in the Western World* (New York: Pantheon, 1956).

Sade, D. A. F. de, *Justine, Philosophy in the Bedroom and Other Writings* (New York: Grove Press, 1965).

Sánchez Vidal, Agustín, *Buñuel, Lorca, Dalí: El enigma sin fin* (Barcelona: Planeta, 1988).

——————— 'De *L'Âge d'or* à *La Ruée vers l'or*', in Bouhours and Schoeller, *L'Âge d'or: Correspondance*.

——————— 'The Andalusian Beasts', in Raeburn (ed.), *Salvador Dalí*.

Stoekl, Allan (ed.), *Visions of Excess: Selected Writings of Georges Bataille 1927–1939* (Manchester: Manchester University Press, 1985).

Weiss, Allen S., 'Between the Sign of the Scorpion and the Sign of the Cross', in his *Aesthetics of Excess* (Albany: State University of New York Press, 1989).

ACKNOWLEDGMENTS
. . . .

For their expertise and amiability, I thank: Montse Agüer and Fèlix Fanés of the Fundació Gala – Salvador Dalí, Figueres; Jean-Michel Bouhours of the Centre Georges Pompidou, Paris; Mariona Bruzzo of the Filmoteca de Catalunya, Barcelona; Emmanuelle Devos of the Cinémathèque Scolaire de la Ville de Paris; Pedro Christian García Buñuel; Thierry Lefebvre; Agustín Sánchez Vidal.

Thanks are also due to Brigitte Berg, Jean-Yves Bériou, Henri Bousquet, Ed Buscombe, Yasha David, Mariàngels Duch, Pablo Fernández, Romà Gubern, Sébastien Guex, Martine Joulia, Montse Jubete, Nick Kimberley, Eric Le Roy, John Lyle, Txema Nogués, Isabelle do O'Gomes, José Pierre, Emilia Pomés, Juan Gabriel Tharrats, Marián Torrens-Alzu, Bernard Weigel, Philip West.

ALSO PUBLISHED

If you would like further information about future BFI Film Classics or about other books on film, media and popular culture from BFI Publishing, please write to:

BFI Film Classics
BFI Publishing
21 Stephen Street
London W1P 2LN

**BFI Film Classics '... could scarcely be
improved upon ... informative, intelligent,
jargon-free companions.'**
The Observer

Each book in the BFI Publishing Film Classics series honours a great film from the history of world cinema. With new titles published each year, the series is rapidly building into a collection representing some of the best writing on film. If you would like to receive further information about future Film Classics or about other books on film, media and popular culture from BFI Publishing, please fill in your name and address and return this card to the BFI*.

No stamp is needed if posted in the UK, Channel Islands, or Isle of Man.

NAME

ADDRESS

POSTCODE

*North America: Please return your card to:
Indiana University Press, Attn: LPB, 601 N Morton Street,
Bloomington, IN 47401-3797

BFI Publishing
21 Stephen Street
FREEPOST 7
LONDON
W1E 4AN